UNCONVENTIONAL
WISDOM

The Economist Explains

ADVENTURES in the
SURPRISINGLY TRUE

Edited by

TOM STANDAGE

D1328831

The
Economist   BOOKS

Published in 2020 under exclusive licence from The Economist by
Profile Books Ltd
29 Cloth Fair
London EC1A 7JQ
www.profilebooks.com

Typeset in Milo by MacGuru Ltd

Printed and bound in Great Britain by CPI Group (UK) Ltd, Croydon CRO 4YY

A CIP catalogue record for this book is available from the British Library

ISBN 978 1 78816 613 3
eISBN 978 1 78283 751 0

Contents

Introduction: in praise of unconventional wisdom

THE CONVENTIONAL WISDOM – that body of knowledge that is generally assumed to be true – has its limits. It is certainly incomplete; it can be out of date; it may contain errors. The wise man, as Socrates put it, is he who knows what he does not know, and thus understands that his wisdom has limits. So it is with the conventional wisdom. Rather than pretending that it is perfect, it is surely better to acknowledge that it has flaws, and strive to address them by extending, maintaining and updating it.

That is where unconventional wisdom comes in, in the form of new knowledge, unexpected findings and deeper explanations of what is already understood – which can only be found by venturing beyond the intellectual frontier of what is already known. The resulting discoveries are often surprising, exciting and counter-intuitive. They may also be incorrect. Unconventional wisdom must be tested carefully against the conventional kind. But where it passes that test, it can be gradually integrated into the body of conventional wisdom as it becomes more widely known and accepted. And then the cycle continues.

This book is a collection of reports from beyond that boundary of accepted knowledge, on a wide range of topics, drawn from *The Economist*'s output of explainers and charts. It brings together new findings and explanations that are not merely surprising, but that also, as far as we can tell, happen to be true. And knowledge that is surprisingly true, though it starts out as unconventional wisdom, is destined to end up becoming widely accepted as conventional wisdom.

So join us on our adventures in some of the wilder reaches of the surprisingly true. For anyone interested in how our understanding of the world is changing, this is the place to look: beyond the limits of knowledge, where old certainties are challenged and new and unexpected ideas are jostling for acceptance. Why, for example, does height matter in politics? Why is it better for the planet for you to be a part-time vegan than a full-time vegetarian? Do friends prefer sloppily wrapped Christmas gifts? Does cannabis really give you the munchies? Should your dog fear Easter more than fireworks night?

By keeping an eye on the places where unconventional wisdom is emerging, you can see what is coming next, and watch the conventional wisdom of the future taking shape. In the process, you can steal a march on other people who are not paying such close attention. Unconventional wisdom encourages you to challenge your preconceptions. It invites you to look more deeply into how the world works. And as well as being informative, it is often amusing or entertaining. We hope you will find that the same is true of this book.

Tom Standage
Deputy Editor, *The Economist*
June 2020

Unconventional wisdom: adventures in the surprisingly true

How pregnancy makes people more law-abiding

Almost any parent will agree that once you have a child, life is never quite the same again. Having to provide for another, utterly dependent, human being can spur new mums and dads to find reserves of generosity, care and energy they never knew they had. Their behaviour changes before the birth, too. A paper entitled "Family formation and crime", published in February 2020 by Maxim Massenkoff and Evan Rose, two economics PhD students at the University of California, Berkeley, suggests that before a child is born, the prospect of impending parenthood makes people much more law-abiding.

Using data on more than 1m babies born in Washington state between 1996 and 2009, and records of thousands of crimes committed there between 1992 and 2015, the authors find that when women become pregnant, they are much less likely to be arrested, for a wide range of crimes. The effect is most marked for "economic" crimes, such as theft and burglary, but is also true of assaults, vandalism, and alcohol and drug offences. Arrest rates fall by 50% almost as soon as women become pregnant and fall much further as the pregnancy goes on. Although they bounce back somewhat after childbirth, arrest rates stabilise at about half pre-pregnancy levels.

More surprisingly, the same pattern holds for fathers. Men are much likelier than women to commit crimes of all sorts in the first place, and the decline in some types of crime is less dramatic for dads than for mums. But arrest rates drop by around 25% once their partners become pregnant, and stay around this mark even after birth. In a blog post commenting on the paper, Alexander Tabarrok of George Mason University described the effect as "astoundingly large". A study by Mr Tabarrok published in 2007 concluded that the threat of an additional 20 years of prison made criminals 17% less likely to reoffend; the prospect of fatherhood, it seems, is more salutary than that of two decades of incarceration.

Alas, Mr Massenkoff and Mr Rose also reach other, less encouraging, conclusions. Arrests of men for domestic violence soar immediately after birth. The authors suggest this may be because new parents are living together for the first time. Whatever the cause, for some, parenthood can bring misery as well as joy.

How much does being haunted reduce a house's value?

Haunted houses are not for the faint of heart. Deceased former tenants – normally those who have suffered violent, untimely deaths – are said to remain in residence. Living occupants may complain of creaking doors and floorboards, shifting furniture, and of hearing knocking sounds, footsteps or voices. Ghostly apparitions may terrorise children; pets flee eerie spectres.

Sceptics might write off such claims as the product of paranoia or an overactive imagination, but haunted houses do spook the property market. That ghosts depress prices, especially in some Asian cities such as Hong Kong, has long been recognised. But a working paper published in 2019 by Utpal Bhattacharya and Kasper Meisner Nielsen of the Hong Kong University of Science and Technology, and Daisy Huang of Nanjing Audit University, attempts to calculate the size of the ectoplasmic discount. It estimates that Hong Kong properties that are considered to be haunted – owing to the unnatural death of a former inhabitant from an accident, murder or suicide – lose a fifth of their value on average. The price of such *hongza*, or haunted flats, can remain depressed for years.

Using a database of more than 1.1m residential real-estate transactions, combined with data from four commercial haunted-house websites (including that maintained by squarefoot.com.hk), the authors identify 898 haunted properties that changed hands between 2000 and 2015. After controlling for size and age, long-term price trends and seasonal fluctuations in demand, they find not only that the price of haunted flats is depressed by an average of 20%, but that there is also a clear "ripple effect" in the local market. Neighbouring properties fall by 5%; those in the same block drop by 3%; and those in the same housing complex by 1%.

So ghosts and ghouls are a factor for discerning Hong Kong house-hunters to weigh. But the process by which a property becomes haunted matters, too. Suicides (which account for nearly three-quarters of hauntings in the territory) reduce the value of

Ghost-benefit analysis
Hong Kong, estimated effect of "haunted" houses on property sale prices*, %

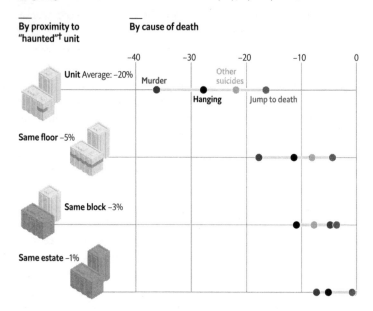

By proximity to "haunted"† unit

By cause of death

Source: "Spillovers in asset prices: the curious case of haunted houses",
U. Bhattacharaya, D. Huang and K. Meisner Nielsen,
HKUST Institute for Emerging Market Studies, working paper, 2019

*2000–15
†Due to an unnatural death

affected properties by between 16% and 28%, depending on the method used; deadly accidents depress prices by 20%. Murders, meanwhile, have the most chilling effect on values, sending prices tumbling by a whopping 36%. But look on the bright side: bargains are available for long-term buyers who have the psychological fortitude to ignore the gruesome history of their prospective purchase – or are willing to ignore things going bump in the night.

The link between air pollution and violent crime

Air pollution is nothing to sniff at. Perhaps a third of all deaths from strokes, lung cancer and respiratory diseases can be linked to toxic air. In some cities, breathing outdoors is as dangerous as smoking 25 cigarettes a day. But whereas the health problems associated with air pollution can take years to manifest themselves, research highlights a much more immediate – and violent – risk.

Breathing dirty air is linked to aggressive behaviour, according to a paper published in 2019 by Jesse Burkhardt and his colleagues at Colorado State University and the University of Minnesota. Using crime data from the Federal Bureau of Investigation and air-pollution data from the Environmental Protection Agency, the authors analyse the link between air pollution and violent crime in 397 American counties between 2006 and 2013.

They find that a 10% increase in same-day exposure to $PM_{2.5}$ (particulate matter less than 2.5 microns in diameter) is associated with a 0.14% increase in violent crimes, such as assault. An equivalent increase in exposure to ozone, an air pollutant, is associated with a 0.3% jump in such crimes. Pollution levels can easily rise by much more than that. In November 2018, owing to wildfires, $PM_{2.5}$ levels in San Francisco reached seven times the usual average. Correlation is not causation, of course (there may, for example, be a third variable affecting both pollution and crime), and the authors are cautious not to speculate about the precise mechanism by which contaminated air might lead to more rapes or robberies.

But this is not the first time researchers have identified a relationship between pollution and crime. In the 1970s, America banned lead-based paint and began phasing out leaded petrol; two decades later, crime fell. Many researchers have since argued that the two developments were linked. In a paper published in 2007, Jessica Wolpaw Reyes, an economist at Amherst College, estimated that the drop in lead exposure experienced by American children in the 1970s and 1980s could explain more than half of the decline in violent crime during the 1990s.

The findings of Mr Burkhardt and his co-authors suggest that cleaner air could reduce violent crime still further. The benefits would be substantial. The authors estimate that a 10% reduction in daily $PM_{2.5}$ and ozone exposure could save America $1.4bn a year through reduced assaults (the savings range from the cost of the immediate police response to lost productivity due to injuries). A lot of people get angry about pollution. Evidently they may get angry because of it, too.

Why Easter is dangerous for dogs

Easter-egg hunts are a delight for children, a pain for parents to organise – and potentially lethal for the family pooch. The worst a chocolate binge can do for a mischievous four-year-old child is a dizzying sugar high. For dogs, however, the theobromine found in cocoa beans can cause vomiting, diarrhoea and seizures. A study published in 2017 of British veterinarian clinics between 2012 and 2017 found a large spike in canine chocolate intoxication in the weeks around Easter. Some 60% of British vets reported such a case in 2018. A similar problem occurs at Christmas.

Peaks of chocolate exposure around Valentine's Day and Halloween, found in previous studies carried out in Germany and America, were not found in Britain, "perhaps reflecting alternative romantic gift choices, or more fastidious curation by their recipient", the researchers noted. Instead, Britain's specific seasonal pattern "merits highlighting this risk to clients, particularly in the run-up to Christmas and Easter", they concluded. No particular breed was associated with risk, but younger dogs (less than four years old) were found to be most likely to have a sweet tooth.

Toxic choc syndrome
Britain, vet consultations per week for dogs with chocolate intoxication, 2012–17 average

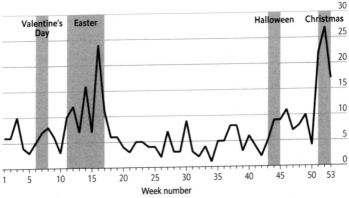

Source: "Heightened risk of canine chocolate exposure at Christmas and Easter", P.-J.M. Noble *et al.*, *Veterinary Record*, 2017

Fortunately, all of the poorly pets in the sample responded to treatment and recovered from their snack-induced ailments. But owners should beware: a pup with a sweet tooth will stop at nothing to get its fill. The study's authors reported examples of dogs slurping chocolate liqueurs and cups of cocoa. Chocolate oranges and Toblerone bars were especially popular, with one naughty pooch guzzling six of both. The worst offender managed to consume an entire "garden of Easter eggs hidden for a large party of small children". Pity the parents who had to deal with the consequences.

Why societies change their minds faster than people do

As recently as the late 1980s, most Americans thought gay sex was not only immoral but also ought to be illegal. Yet by 2015, when the Supreme Court legalised same-sex marriage, there were only faint murmurs of protest. Today, two-thirds of Americans support it, and even those who frown on it make no serious effort to criminalise it.

This surge in tolerance illustrates how fast public opinion can shift. The change occurred because two trends reinforced each other. First, many socially conservative old people have died, and their places in polling samples have been taken by liberal millennials. In addition, some people changed their minds. Support for gay marriage has risen by some 30 percentage points within each generation since 2004, from 20% to 49% among those born between 1928 and 1945 and from 45% to 78% among those born after 1980. But this shift in opinion makes gay marriage an exception among political issues. Since 1972 the University of Chicago has run a General Social Survey every year or two, which asks Americans their views on a wide range of topics. Over time, public opinion has grown more liberal. But this is mostly the result of generational replacement, not of changes of heart.

For example, in 1972, 42% of Americans said communist books should be banned from public libraries. Views varied widely by age: 55% of people born before 1928 (who were 45 or older at the time) supported a ban, compared with 37% of people aged 27 to 44 and just 25% of those aged 26 or younger. Today only a quarter of Americans favour this policy. However, within each of these birth cohorts, views today are almost identical to those from 47 years ago. The change was caused entirely by generational replacement, with the share of respondents born before 1928 falling from 49% to nil, and that of millennials – who were not born until at least 1981, and staunchly oppose such a ban – rising from zero to 36%.

Not every issue is as extreme as these two. But on six of the eight questions for which the data were analysed by *The Economist*

On most issues, public opinion changes mainly as younger generations replace older ones

United States, % agreeing by generation   •••••• National average

Communist books should be removed from public libraries

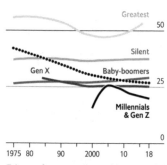

Tolerance for communist speech has risen solely because older generations have died off

Abortion should be allowed for any reason

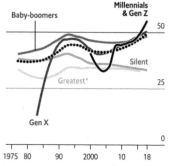

Until recently, boomers were more pro-choice than both their parents and their children were

The government spends too little on improving black people's lives

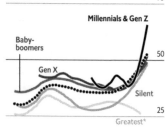

The share of people who think minority groups suffer from injustice has surged since 2013

Sources: General Social Survey; *The Economist*

Gay people should be allowed to get married

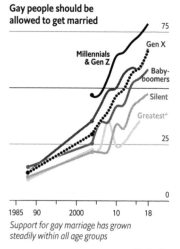

Support for gay marriage has grown steadily within all age groups

*And earlier

"Greatest" generation
Born before 1928

Silent generation
Born 1928–45

Baby-boomers
Born 1946–64

Generation X
Born 1965–80

Millennials and Generation Z
Born after 1980

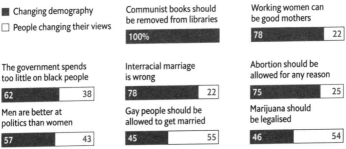

Share of change in opinion explained by:

■ Changing demography
☐ People changing their views

Communist books should be removed from libraries
100%

Working women can be good mothers
78 | 22

The government spends too little on black people
62 | 38

Interracial marriage is wrong
78 | 22

Abortion should be allowed for any reason
75 | 25

Men are better at politics than women
57 | 43

Gay people should be allowed to get married
45 | 55

Marijuana should be legalised
46 | 54

*And earlier

– all save gay marriage and marijuana legalisation – demographic shifts accounted for a bigger share of overall movement in public opinion than changes in beliefs within cohorts. On average, their impact was about twice as large. Social activists devote themselves to changing people's views, and sometimes succeed. In general, however, battles for hearts and minds are won by grinding attrition more often than by rapid conquest.

Are extraterrestrials extra patriotic?

In the final scene of *Independence Day*, a blockbuster film from 1996, Captain Steve Hiller (Will Smith), who has just saved the world from alien annihilation, watches as exploding debris from an extraterrestrial mothership lights up the sky, just in time for the American holiday. Turning to his stepson, he says with a smile, "Didn't I promise you fireworks?" For Americans, such pyrotechnic displays are an important Fourth of July tradition. Can the same be said for UFOs?

Perhaps. According to the National UFO Reporting Centre (NUFORC), an American non-profit organisation that has collected reports of unidentified flying objects since 1974, UFO sightings tend to spike on July 4th. Between 1995 and 2018, around 2% of all sightings recorded by NUFORC fell on this date – seven times more than would be expected by chance. What, other than an other-worldly surge of American patriotism among extraterrestrials, could explain this strange phenomenon?

Hollywood may be partly to blame. In the two years before the release of the Will Smith film, NUFORC recorded an average of seven UFO sightings on July 4th (eight in 1995 and six in 1996). In 1997, a year after aliens burst onto the big screen, there were 74 – more than ten times as many. Traditions associated with the July 4th holiday may also help explain the spike. Independence Day is typically spent outdoors. Heavy alcohol use is not uncommon. Intoxication may cause some people to confuse celebratory fireworks with alien spacecraft.

UFO sightings cannot be blamed entirely on drunkenness. They often have earthly explanations. Some of the biggest spikes in reported UFO sightings in recent years have later been explained by meteors (such as that observed in the Midwest in November 1999), missiles (such as a US Navy launch in November 2015) or debris from satellites re-entering the atmosphere. Or so the government would have you believe.

What waffle restaurants reveal about hurricanes

Waffle House, a breakfast chain from the American South, is better known for reliability than quality. All its restaurants stay open every hour of every day. After extreme weather, such as floods, tornadoes and hurricanes, Waffle Houses are quick to reopen, even if they can serve only a limited menu. That makes them a remarkably reliable, if informal, barometer for weather damage. In 2011, both the Waffle House restaurants near Joplin, Missouri stayed open during a devastating tornado that killed 158 people and caused $3bn in damage. Because of that, government officials responding to hurricanes have taken to monitoring the so-called "Waffle House Index".

The index was invented by Craig Fugate, a former director of the Federal Emergency Management Agency (FEMA) in 2004 after a spate of hurricanes battered America's east coast. "If a Waffle House is closed because there's a disaster, it's bad. We call it red. If they're open but have a limited menu, that's yellow," he explained to NPR, America's public radio network. Fully functioning restaurants are tagged in the Waffle House Index in shining green. The company is leaning into its reputation. When a dangerous hurricane approaches, the firm activates a Waffle House Storm Centre to monitor it and provide guidance to its restaurant managers.

A blog post from FEMA, published in 2011, explained why the index is not merely endearing, but also informative: "The sooner restaurants, grocery and corner stores, or banks can reopen, the sooner local economies will start generating revenue again – signalling a stronger recovery for that community." Though the first-order effect of hurricanes is the destruction of homes and displacement of people, they can also prove devastating to local economies. New Orleans lost more than half its population after Hurricane Katrina in 2005 – and 40% of its jobs. So the Waffle House Index provides an indicator of economic resilience.

Climate scientists think that a warming planet makes for

more frequent and more destructive hurricanes. Humanity's unhelpful tendency to build homes and cities along coastlines does not help matters. Swiss Re, an insurance firm, estimates that global disasters inflicted $140bn in economic losses in 2019. With countries shuffling their feet on emissions reductions, it is likely that disasters will only become more costly – because not every business is as hardy as America's indomitable waffle chain.

Why friends prefer sloppily wrapped Christmas gifts

During a gap year in England in 2002, Jessica Rixom, an American student, earned extra pocket money gift-wrapping sweets at Thorntons, a British chocolate-maker. When she returned to America, she wondered if her knack for wrapping would score her points with friends and family. In fact, it may have done the opposite. A paper published in 2019 by Ms Rixom, now a professor of marketing at the University of Nevada, Reno, concludes that slick parcel-packing can actually be a turn-off.

The finding defies conventional wisdom. Previous research has shown that fancy wrapping paper summons happy memories, making recipients more fond of their gifts. Yet, according to Ms Rixom and her co-authors, Brett Rixom and Erick Mas of Vanderbilt University, such positive feelings may materialise only when giving gifts to people we do not know all that well. With acquaintances, they argue, effort put into wrapping is taken as a signal of the value of the relationship, making the gift more meaningful. With close friends, however, the opposite is true. In an established relationship, wrapping paper sends a signal about the value of the gift itself. A neat package raises expectations – which then become harder to meet.

The authors conducted three experiments in which they asked subjects to rate their feelings about gifts that were either neatly or sloppily wrapped, from one (for displeased) to nine (for delighted), and then unwrap the gift in question and rate it. The first two experiments (the first involving gift-wrapped mugs, and the second involving a set of headphones) found that people were, on average, happier with sloppily wrapped gifts, seemingly because their expectations were lower. In a third experiment Ms Rixom and her colleagues recruited 261 adults from Mechanical Turk, an online crowd-working platform. Subjects were shown images of a gift, either neatly or sloppily wrapped, and were asked to imagine receiving it from either a friend or an acquaintance. They found that, when received from an acquaintance, neatly wrapped gifts were more highly rated than sloppily wrapped ones (6.7 v 3.8, respectively). Coming from a friend, however, sloppy parcels were rated more highly than tidy ones (6.5 v 4.4).

Holiday gift-givers should therefore consider the nature of their relationship with recipients when prepping presents, says Ms Rixom. "It's about taking a step back and asking who are you wrapping this gift for: a friend, or just an acquaintance?" Each year Britons tear through an estimated 365,000 kilometres of festive wrapping during the holidays, and Americans spend a whopping $2.6bn on the stuff. To avoid raising expectations, they might wish to wrap presents sloppily for their closest friends, perhaps using newspaper instead. For their part, companies like IG Design Group, the world's biggest producer of wrapping paper, might prefer to keep this finding under wraps.

Globally curious: particular propensities from around the world

Which countries spend the most on pets?

Americans adore their pets. Roughly two in three households own one, according to the American Pet Products Association, a trade group. Dogs are loved most of all: they outnumber cats by about five to four, according to GfK, a market-research firm. Nowhere is America's devotion to dogs more evident than at the Westminster Kennel Club Dog Show, which takes place every year in New York. At the 2020 show, more than 2,600 dogs were clipped, washed and blow-dried by their doting handlers in the hopes of taking home the coveted best-in-show title. Cost is no object for these pampered pooches. By one estimate, caring for a top show dog can set you back more than $250,000 a year.

The pet industry is booming beyond the world of competitions. According to Euromonitor International, a research firm, the pet-care market grew by more than 66% between 2009 and 2019, while the global economy expanded by just 43%. Americans spent more than $52bn on their pets in 2019, up from $34bn in 2009. Most of that went on food, but more than $18bn was spent on pet supplies and accessories. On a per-person basis, no other country comes close to splashing out as much as America on such products. Britain spent $93 per person last year, on average, while France shelled out $87.

What accounts for the sector's howling success? As people grow wealthier, their attitudes to domestic animals tend to change. A poll conducted in 2015 found that 95% of American pet owners considered their animals to be full members of the family – up from 88% in 2007. It is little wonder owners are spending money on their furry companions. And the range of pet products available today extends far beyond food, to exercise wheels for cats and designer clothes for dogs. Barbour, a posh British outdoor-clothing brand, sells a range of fetching jackets and accessories for dogs. If your pooch likes the finer things in life, you can treat it to a luxury collar from Louis Vuitton – a steal at just under $400.

With so much money being spent on pets, you might suppose

Reigning cats and dogs

Pet ownership by country
2016, % of households

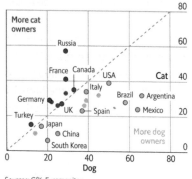

Pet-care spending per person
2019, $

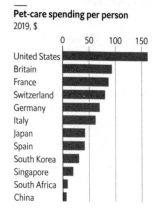

Sources: GfK; Euromonitor

that some would trickle down to the prize-winning pooches at competitions like the Westminster. But competitors are not in it for the money: no cash prizes are awarded to dogs or their owners. In the dog-eat-dog world of competitive canines, you'd think they might throw a dog a bone.

Which countries offer the biggest fuel subsidies?

A crisis was defused in Quito, Ecuador's capital, in October 2019. After 11 days of mass protests, which left at least seven dead and more than 1,000 injured, President Lenín Moreno's government agreed not to scrap subsidies on petrol and diesel. Repeal of the popular subsidies, which cost the government an estimated $1.3bn a year, was part of a package of public-spending cuts needed to secure a $4.2bn loan from the IMF. Promises to soften the blow by increasing welfare payments to poor families failed to quell the uprising.

It is little wonder that Mr Moreno's decision to end subsidies sparked unrest. Ecuador has subsidised the cost of fuel for 40 years. According to the Inter-American Development Bank, the subsidies have gobbled up 7% of the country's yearly spending over the past decade. Although they benefit poor Ecuadorians, better-off households gain the most. As a way of redistributing income, they are remarkably inefficient. One study found that using petrol subsidies to transfer $1 to the poorest fifth of households cost the government $20. It would make far more sense simply to give them cash.

Costly as fuel subsidies are to Ecuador, plenty of countries (including many big energy producers) spend far more of their national income in this way. These include two other Latin American governments, with spendthrift Venezuela far outstripping the field. In all, governments around the world blew $427bn in 2018, according to the International Energy Agency, a Paris-based inter-governmental think-tank. (Venezuela finally reduced its fuel subsidies in June 2020, allowing drivers to buy 120 litres a month for $0.02, and $0.50 thereafter.)

Such "pre-tax" measures of the cost of subsidies are based on the difference between the price paid by consumers and the cost to the state of supplying fuel. A broader "post-tax" measure, based on the difference between consumer prices and estimates of efficient prices (taking into account environmental damage, traffic accidents and so forth), yields even higher numbers. The IMF puts the post-tax cost of energy subsidies in Ecuador at three times the fiscal cost, for example. Governments rarely succeed in getting rid of subsidies. Social unrest in Bolivia in 2010, Nigeria in 2012 and Sudan in 2013 were all sparked by energy reforms.

Why so many Latin Americans want to emigrate

When people vote with their feet, they usually make an informed choice. Venezuelans, for example, have many compelling reasons to leave Venezuela. Its government admits that it killed 5,287 people in 2018 for "resistance to authority", inflation has reached as high as 2,700,000%, and the average person has lost 11kg (24lb) from hunger. Perhaps around 13% of the population have fled – more than 4m people. Citizens of El Salvador, Honduras and Guatemala have also been emigrating en masse. They are fed up with poverty and violence, and people-smugglers have become adept at transporting them. This exodus was the main reason why officers at the United States' southern border detained more people trying to cross in the year to July 2019 than in any 12-month period since 2009.

Venezuela and Central America are uniquely troubled. But their citizens' desire to get out is increasingly common. Gallup, a pollster, asks people in 120 countries each year if they want to emigrate. From 2010 to 2018 the share that said "yes" rose in 15 of the 19 Latin American nations it tracks. In 2010, 19% of people in the region hoped to move abroad permanently, the same as in Europe. Now 31% do, as many as in the Middle East and Africa.

Many are afraid of being killed. In Brazil, murders hit a record high of 63,880 in 2017, following a resurgence of fighting between criminal gangs. The share of citizens who wish to emigrate tripled to 33%. The country's homicide rate is now roughly level with Colombia's – where it fell as the government's war with the FARC guerrillas wound down. In countries where crime has not risen, economic doldrums have been the main driver of discontent. In 2010, Latin America's GDP grew by 6%, well above the global average. By 2016 it was shrinking, due to recessions in Brazil and Argentina. In Mexico, the region's second-biggest country, the economy has plodded along with low productivity growth and little social mobility.

Another thing making Latin America less liveable is corruption. The region is grubbier than you would expect, given its relative affluence. In Brazil the Lava Jato investigation has exposed bribes paid by industrial firms to scores of politicians. Alan García, a former president of Peru, killed himself in April 2019 to avoid arrest in conjunction with the Brazilian scandal. According to Latinobarómetro, an annual survey, the share of Latin Americans dissatisfied with how democracy works in their country rose from 52% in 2010 to 71% in 2018. Latin Americans are not just voting with their feet; they are venting at the ballot box, too. In 2018 messianic populists who railed against corruption and crime won presidential elections in Brazil (the conservative Jair Bolsonaro) and Mexico (the leftist Andrés Manuel López Obrador). If voters remain this disenchanted, more leaders with autocratic streaks are likely to follow.

Why West Africa has become the world's new piracy hotspot

Compared with their counterparts in Somalia, the pirates prowling the Gulf of Guinea have attracted relatively little global attention. That may now be changing. A report by One Earth Future, an NGO, says that the region experienced more incidents of piracy in 2018 than anywhere else in the world. The report adds to a growing chorus of international concern about West Africa's piracy problem. A shipowners' association has called for the deployment of international navies to the region. India has banned its citizens from working as sailors in the Gulf of Guinea. Maritime-security experts advise ships travelling to the region to wrap their decks in razor wire or hire local naval escorts.

Such concern is justified. West Africa's pirates are much deadlier than those in Asia or Latin America. In the latter two regions, most piracy takes the form of petty theft: someone clambers aboard a ship docked at port to swipe a few items or mug a sailor. West African pirates used to specialise in stealing oil from tankers. But since 2014, when oil prices plummeted, they have copied their Somali counterparts and focused on kidnapping crews for ransom. They no longer prey exclusively on oil tankers. In 2018 they are believed to have kidnapped almost 200 people.

West Africa's pirates may also be harder to stop than those elsewhere. Off Somalia, where the government controlled little of the country's territory, international navies were given free rein and shipowners could hire private armed guards. Although pirates still occasionally probe the waters off Somalia for a vulnerable ship, they have largely been kept at bay. In South-East Asia, where the coastal states are richer and better run, governments have curbed piracy by working together and sharing intelligence. Better policing at ports has also led to a fall in petty theft in recent years.

West Africa lies awkwardly between the two. Most of its pirates are from the poor and lawless Niger Delta region of Nigeria. The Nigerian government is more functional than Somalia's and would resent foreign ships or private guards in its waters. But it has its hands full with insurgencies, banditry and local conflict on land. Its navy is thinly spread and ill equipped. Until the Delta is better governed, do not expect the pirates to disappear from the seas off West Africa.

Why the United Nations reduced its global population forecasts

The United Nations is the world's most important watcher of human tides. Its demographers have a good record of predicting global population change, although they have made mistakes about individual countries. So it is worth paying attention when the UN revises its figures, as it does every few years. The latest bulletin, released in June 2019, is especially surprising. Previous revisions have sent the projected global population upwards. The latest one cuts it back. The UN now thinks the world will contain a little over 9.7bn people in 2050 and just under 10.9bn in 2100. The first figure is 37m lower than the UN forecast two years ago. The latter is 309m lower – almost an America's worth of people revised away. Why did the UN reduce its forecasts?

One reason is that birth rates are falling faster than expected in some developing countries. In the late 1980s Kenya had a fertility rate of 6.5, implying a woman could expect to have that many children. Two years ago the UN reckoned Kenya's fertility rate would drop to 2.1 (the point at which the population sustains itself without growing) only in the late 2070s. Because of new data, it now thinks Kenya will reach that point a decade earlier. Uganda also looks less fecund. A smaller cut to India's fertility rate has a big effect on the global population forecasts because India has so many people.

The UN's population model assumes that countries with fertility rates well below two will bounce back a little. Even in countries where babies have become rare, most people continue to believe that the ideal family contains two or even three kids. But the recovery keeps failing to happen in some places, so the demographers have changed their forecasts in a second way. They now expect some countries with extremely low birth rates, such as Italy, Japan and South Korea, to stay that way for years. South Korea, which has a fertility rate of just 1.1, is now expected to have 30m people in 2100 – down from 51m today.

This century, Africa will replace Asia as the driver of population growth

Global population projections, by region, bn

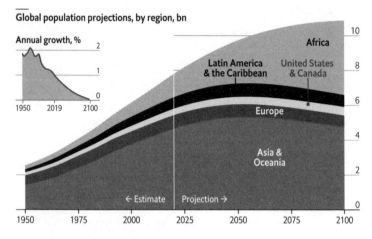

Annual growth, %

Birth rates have fallen everywhere, faster than they did in the West

Total fertility rate, children per woman
Years from high fertility (around 6) to replacement fertility (around 2.1) --- Projection

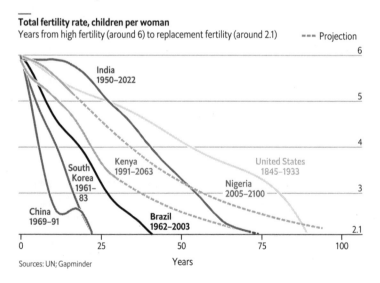

Sources: UN; Gapminder

Years

Another change has to do with death. Most people are living longer. The biggest improvement is in Eastern Africa and Southern Africa, where HIV is being treated better. In America, however, the opioid epidemic has pushed up the death rate, especially for men. The chance of a 15-year-old boy dying by the age of 50 is now higher in America than it is in Bangladesh. It would be welcome if the American forecast, at least, proved to be too pessimistic.

Which country has the biggest bullshitters?

Everybody tells the occasional fib. But whereas liars consciously conceal the truth, reckons Harry Frankfurt, a philosopher, bullshitters are shameless: they say what they want to, without even considering the truth. Bluffers seem to be everywhere: the share of Americans who believe that most people can be trusted has fallen from 48% in 1984 to just 31% today.

The latest study of the phenomenon has found that people in North America are especially prone to talking bull. John Jerrim and Nikki Shure, of University College London's Institute of Education, and Phil Parker of the Australian Catholic University used an educational survey of 40,000 teenage students from nine English-speaking countries to find out who is most likely to spout nonsense. They inserted a section into the questionnaire which asked students how well they understood a collection of 16 mathematical concepts. Some of these were familiar, such as "polygon" and "probability", but three were fake: "proper number", "subjunctive scaling" and "declarative fraction".

Call my bluff

Standard deviations from average bullshit score, measuring truthfulness among 15-year-olds on a maths test

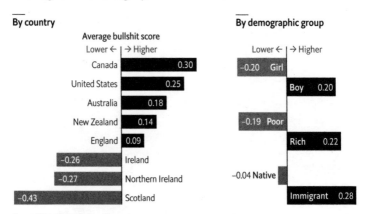

By country

Average bullshit score
Lower ← | → Higher

Canada	0.30
United States	0.25
Australia	0.18
New Zealand	0.14
England	0.09
Ireland	−0.26
Northern Ireland	−0.27
Scotland	−0.43

By demographic group

Lower ← | → Higher

Girl	−0.20
Boy	0.20
Poor	−0.19
Rich	0.22
Native	−0.04
Immigrant	0.28

Source: IZA Institute of Labour Economics

The results showed substantial differences between countries. Canadian and American teenagers were especially likely to profess knowledge of these bogus topics, whereas the Scots and Irish were perfectly happy to admit their ignorance. In news that will shock nobody, in every country boys claimed to be experts more often than girls. The rich were more boastful than the poor. More surprising was the finding that immigrants were generally more likely to bluff about maths than native students were.

What explains these differences? The academics doubt that the bullshitters were simply trying to impress the questionnaire's markers. The students who bluffed about maths were just as likely as the non-bluffers to admit that they had skipped school recently, for example. A more likely answer is that the blaggers overestimated their own knowledge. They also tended to rate themselves highly when it came to gauging their own popularity, their perseverance in academic tasks and their problem-solving ability. The data suggest that they might not be consciously lying, but may instead be weaving their own fantasies.

How long does it take for country name-changes to take hold?

What's in a name? On January 25th 2019, after months of negotiations, lawmakers in Greece voted to recognise its northern neighbour Macedonia as "North Macedonia", thus ending a 28-year-old dispute with the tiny Balkan nation and paving the way for NATO and EU membership. The outcome was hailed as a historic achievement. But Macedonia is not the only country to have changed its name lately. In 2016, the Czech Republic adopted "Czechia" as the official short version of its name. And in 2018 the African kingdom of Swaziland was renamed "eSwatini" by its all-powerful monarch.

Countries change their names for a variety of historical and cultural reasons. In North Macedonia's case, the goal was to settle rival claims over a name that dates back to the ancient kingdom of Alexander the Great. For eSwatini, the aim was to move beyond its colonial past and assert an African identity – it had previously been one of the handful of African countries that chose to keep the name used by its European colonisers after gaining independence. Czechia's objective was far more practical. The country hopes that the snappier name will be better suited for informal use, in the same way that "Slovakia" is used for the Slovak Republic.

Alas, new country names can be slow to catch on. A look back at some of the most significant such changes of the 20th century using data from Google Ngram Viewer, a database of over 5m printed works, suggests it can take years for a new name to gain widespread usage. After the former British colony of Ceylon adopted the name Sri Lanka in 1972, it took nearly a decade for the new name to gain more literary mentions than its predecessor. The name Zimbabwe surpassed Rhodesia in about half that time. When Burma's ruling military junta changed the country's name to Myanmar in 1989, some foreign governments were reluctant to acknowledge the change, on the basis that doing so could be seen as granting the regime legitimacy. By 2008, the name Burma was still being mentioned in English-language books more than twice as often as Myanmar.

Whether North Macedonia will win over the public remains to be seen. Change takes time. But within a few years the acrimonious dispute over the name of the kingdom once ruled by Alexander the Great will, with luck, have finally passed into history.

What's the point of twin cities?

Welcome to Brussels – twinned with Atlanta, Ljubljana and Prague. Like so many other big cities, small towns and even obscure villages, the Belgian capital has acquired a number of symbolic siblings over the past half-century. Yet it isn't always clear what the purpose of such relationships is. By some counts the first twinning took place in 836, when Le Mans in France handed over the relics of St Liborius to Paderborn in Germany, to shore up the influence of Charlemagne. In its more recent iteration, twinning took off in Europe and the United States after the second world war. But is this linking of towns outdated, something to be wondered at merely by those passing the signs that greet drivers entering a town?

In the beginning, town-twinning was idealistic and chummy. Often pairings were the result of mayors who were mates. But there was also genuine interest in transnational reconciliation. By connecting citizens through school exchanges, food, sport and travel, the process helped peoples who had opposed one another in conflict get to know each other in peacetime. Coventry in Britain and Stalingrad (now Volgograd) in the former Soviet Union, which were damaged to differing degrees during the war, paired up in 1944. Eventually Coventry was twinned with Dresden, another city that suffered badly. Since the collapse of the Soviet Union, the urgency to institutionalise bonds between citizens has been lost. War in Europe has seemed distant, and revolutions in communication and mass travel have allowed people to get to know other countries without mayors acting as middlemen (or women). Recent connections, such as the Scottish village of Dull with Boring in America and Bland Shire in Australia, seem intended only to generate a chuckle.

But look closer, and 21st-century twinning seems to be evolving into something more practical. Cities and regions seeking solutions to social, economic or environmental problems look for comparable communities with which to share their technical expertise. Offers by mayors of towns in the Baltics to share their knowledge of how to make Soviet-era buildings more energy-efficient have been snapped up by mayors in North Macedonia, for example. Nouvelle-Aquitaine in France and Plateau Central in Burkina Faso made the most of their shared tongue to establish a joint programme for sustainable economic development and to fight climate change. León in Nicaragua and Utrecht in the Netherlands got together to plant 500,000 trees when one lacked space and the other lacked money. Inter-city diplomacy has even developed beyond bilateral partnerships into groups such as the C40, an association of large cities committed to dealing with climate change.

Even as these networks and new relationships develop, old-fashioned twinning has not died out. But it is changing from a platform for cultural exchange between citizens of countries separated by war into a way to reconcile citizens whose nations are starting to drift apart. Since the 2016 Brexit vote, interest from British local authorities in setting up partnerships with European towns has apparently increased. Oxford, in Britain, and Wroclaw, in Poland, are one new pairing. They bonded over their dreaming spires and a desire to forge new links across Europe while others are breaking down. In this context, the concept of twinning might find a new lease of life, allowing citizens and local representatives to act as de facto diplomats at a time when relationships between national governments are weakening.

Why people in Senegal will pay so much for sheep

"If I had $100,000, I'd spend it all on sheep," says Abib Seck, a sheep-dealer. Such enthusiasm is not unusual in Senegal. People there adore sheep. Not only are they delicious, they can also be status symbols. Every year during Tabaski, a religious festival, hundreds of thousands of sheep are sacrificed (and then gobbled up). Poorer families often take out crippling loans to buy one so they don't lose social standing.

The latest craze is for a particularly fancy breed. Ladoum sheep are huge and majestic – rams can weigh as much as three grown men. Startlingly, they are also without wool (which is not a problem in West Africa as it is too hot to wear jumpers). Some Ladoum look more like small horses than sheep. They are too valuable to be sacrificed to any god. Instead, dealers sell them to rich folk – businessmen, religious leaders and government ministers – who keep them as pets. They are so popular that there are beauty pageants for them on television with prizes worth thousands of dollars. At an agricultural fair in Dakar, Senegal's capital, well-heeled couples check the pedigree of sheep they see as an investment. Several dealers claim to supply the president of Senegal himself.

Prices for Ladoum sheep have rocketed in recent years. New breeders are flocking to the trade. Mr Seck bought his first three sheep in 2016 for a total of $8,500 and bred them. By 2019 one of their offspring, a huge ram called Cronus, was worth around $70,000. In a country where GDP per head is $1,000, some think such prices are shear madness. But Ladoum-lovers insist they are worth it. "They make me feel happy," says Mr Seck. "The breed has a lot of charisma." He now has over 40 in his home. He employs two men to look after them but still chooses to spend most of his time with them. He says that his wife doesn't mind because the animals are so lucrative. He frequently sells Ladoum lambs for $2,500–5,000. He hopes to buy a separate house for his ovine chums.

Breeding such treasures can be perilous. "[Sheep thieves are] our biggest problem," says Mamadou Touré, another dealer. One night, he says, armed men rammed into his friend's house and stole six ewes worth $85,000. Whether these prices are sustainable remains to be seen. Never mind the lack of wool – once Ladoumania subsides, owners may have to take a haircut on their investment.

If a 13-year-old murders a 10-year-old, is it a crime?

At what age does an illegal act by a child become a crime? A grisly murder in China brought this question to the fore. In October 2019 a 13-year-old boy in Dalian, a city in the north-east, confessed to sexually assaulting a 10-year-old girl, stabbing her to death and dumping her body on the side of a road. The boy is not behind bars, however, because under Chinese law children are not held criminally responsible for their actions until they turn 14. He is instead spending three years in a "rehabilitation centre", the harshest punishment available.

Such a rule is not unusual. The United Nations recommends that countries set their minimum age of criminal responsibility (MACR) no lower than 12, and encourages them to make the limit older. Many do. More than 40 countries set the cut-off at 14. A handful – including Argentina and Mozambique – draw the line at 16. Elsewhere, the minimum age is much younger. India, Pakistan and Bangladesh, among others, set the MACR at seven. In some countries, the age at which children can be charged with crimes varies from place to place. In America, there are 33 states with no minimum at all. In Wisconsin, 10-year-olds may be charged. In other countries, the definition can be fuzzy. In Syria, for example, children are held criminally responsible only if they have reached puberty. Several African countries have similar criteria. In Iran, girls are legally responsible after nine "lunar years" (which, at 354 days, are slightly shorter than ordinary years) but boys have until they are 15.

There are often calls to lower the MACR after an under-age child commits a particularly egregious offence. The murder in China provoked a debate about whether exempting children from prosecution prevents justice from being done. One problem is that, in most legal systems, offenders are not criminally liable if they do not understand they have done something wrong. Determining when a child is capable of having criminal intent can be difficult.

Moreover, most countries, even those with the death penalty, abide by the UN Convention on the Rights of the Child, which forbids capital punishment or life imprisonment for under-18s. But some countries where the death penalty for under-18s is supposedly banned, including Egypt and Iran, have been accused of carrying out executions nonetheless.

Opponents of punishing children argue that youngsters are often victims of circumstance. Many come from poor families or are manipulated or exploited by adults. Criminalising them may only compound these harms, limiting job prospects and encouraging recidivism. Critics also point out that lowering the age of responsibility may not necessarily reduce crime. After Denmark cut it from 15 to 14 in 2010, researchers found that 14-year-olds were no less likely to commit crimes.

Representative selection: political peculiarities

Why height matters in politics

"Mini Mike is a 5'4" mass of dead energy," President Donald Trump tweeted on February 13th 2020. Two days earlier he had sneered at his rival's golf swing: "Mini Mike is a short ball (very) hitter. Tiny club head speed." Mr Trump was, of course, referring to Michael Bloomberg, the former mayor of New York City, who was vying at the time with several other Democratic hopefuls for the party's presidential nomination. The billionaire businessman (who is in fact five-foot-seven) is the latest in an eclectic and ever-lengthening list of supposedly diminutive figures whom Mr Trump (who claims to be six-foot-three) has ridiculed – among them Kim Jong Un, the dictator of North Korea (around five-seven), and Sadiq Khan, the mayor of London (five-five). These jibes are often dismissed as frenzied fits of Twitter-induced rage. Yet there may be a method to Mr Trump's madness.

Presidents are becoming taller relative to average Americans (as measured by army records of recruits of the same age cohort); the last president shorter than this mean was William McKinley, elected in 1896. And there is evidence that being short can hinder a candidate's presidential prospects. A paper published in 2013, by psychologists at the University of Groningen in the Netherlands, analysed the results of American presidential elections dating back to 1789. It found that taller candidates received more votes than shorter ones roughly two-thirds of the time. And the taller the candidates relative to their opponents, the greater the average margin of victory. Among presidents who have sought a second term, winners have been two inches taller, on average, than losers. The authors conclude that height may explain as much as 15% of the variation in election outcomes.

Why do long-limbed politicians outperform their stumpier rivals? The reason may be biological. In the animal kingdom, packs are often led by large males who are more adept at dominating their rivals. But there is a psychological component as well. Taller people enjoy higher self-esteem, on average, and are perceived to be healthier, more intelligent and more authoritative. This may help to account for their advantage at the polls. Causality also seems to run in the opposite direction: popularity can influence perceptions of height. Americans polled in January 1978 estimated that Richard Nixon, who had resigned the presidency in disgrace more than three years earlier, was shorter than Jimmy Carter, who had been elected in 1976. In reality, Nixon was two inches taller.

It is not clear whether height matters as much for female politicians as for male ones. Only one woman has secured a major party's presidential nomination: Hillary Clinton (five-five) secured more votes than Mr Trump in 2016, but lost in the electoral college. Judged on height alone, six-footers Bernie Sanders and Joe Biden were best-placed among the 2020 Democratic hopefuls to beat Mr Trump, which may help explain why they outlasted the rest of the field. But even if Mr Trump is exaggerating his height (analysis of photographs suggests his true height is six-two), there is no doubt that he looked down on all the would-be Democratic challengers – in more ways than one.

How Arabs are losing faith in religious parties and leaders

"No to religion or sect," cry the protesters in Iraq. "No to Islam, no to Christianity, revolt for the nation," echo those in Lebanon. Across the Arab world people have been turning against religious political parties and the clerics who helped bring them to power. Many appear to be giving up on Islam, too.

These trends are reflected in data from Arab Barometer, a pollster that surveys Arab countries. Across the region the share of people expressing much trust in political parties, most of which

---

Faith, less

Selected Arab countries, share of respondents, %   ▉ 2012–14   ▉ 2018–19

Trust in Islamist parties

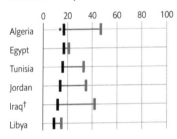

Trust in religious leaders

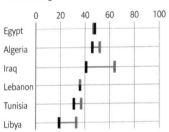

Those who say they are not religious

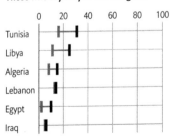

Muslims who say they attend mosque at least some of the time

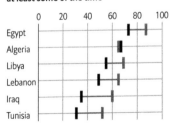

*2016 †2013 survey asked about Muslim Brotherhood and 2019 survey about the Iraqi Islamic Party

Source: Arab Barometer

have a religious tint, fell by well over a third between 2011 and 2018, to 15%. (The share of Iraqis saying they do not trust parties at all rose from 51% to 78%.) The decline in trust for Islamist parties is similarly dramatic, falling from 35% in 2013, when the question was first widely asked, to 20% in 2018.

The doubts extend to religious leaders. In 2013 around 51% of respondents said they trusted their religious leaders to a "great" or "medium" extent. When a comparable question was asked in 2018 the number was down to 40%. The share of Arabs who think religious leaders should have influence over government decision-making is also steadily declining. "State religious actors are often perceived as co-opted by the regime, making citizens unlikely to trust them," says Michael Robbins of Arab Barometer.

The share of Arabs describing themselves as "not religious" has risen to 13%, from 8% in 2013. That includes nearly half of young Tunisians, a third of young Libyans, a quarter of young Algerians and a fifth of young Egyptians. But the numbers are fuzzy. Nearly half of Iraqis described themselves as "religious", up from 39% in 2013. Yet the share who say they attend Friday prayers has fallen by nearly half, to 33%. Perhaps faith is increasingly personal, says Mr Robbins.

Why do countries with more democracy want less of it?

One of the assumptions often made about democracies is that, like fine wine, they get better with age. Citizens of democratic societies grow up learning about the benefits of political freedoms and civil liberties. As adults, they reap the rewards of representative government. The more time a country spends as a democracy, the argument goes, the more the public will support it. But research published in the *American Political Science Review* in February 2020 suggests this presumption may be wrong. Using data on democratic quality as well as public opinion in 135 countries, Christopher Claassen of the University of Glasgow finds that after countries strengthen certain democratic institutions – in particular those intended to protect individual rights and check the power of executives – public support for democracy falls. Conversely, when democracy is weakened, support for it tends to increase.

This phenomenon can be seen most clearly in autocracies and fledgling democracies. After Egypt began experimenting with representative democracy in 2012, following decades of authoritarian rule and a popular revolution sparked by the Arab Spring, public support for democracy fell. A similar story has played out elsewhere. Croatia, Kenya and Peru, for example, all witnessed declines in support for democracy following the introduction of greater political freedoms and liberties. The inverse also holds. After Hugo Chávez began dismantling Venezuela's democratic institutions following his election in 1998, enthusiasm for democracy spiked. It would eventually reach levels found in Scandinavia, where support for democracy is higher than it is in most regions. "It's such a clear effect of people reacting to Chávez undermining democracy," says Dr Claassen, who measured levels of democracy using indices that tracked elements such as the cleanliness of elections, adult enfranchisement and the protection of individual and minority rights.

This relationship emerges in countries with long-established democracies, too. As America's democracy strengthened in the early 2000s, public support dipped. In the past few years, as measures of liberal democracy in America have declined slightly, support has edged back up. Increases in electoral representation of and participation by women and minorities have tended to increase America's rankings in international democracy tables over the years. Recent attacks on judicial independence and growing polarisation have lowered its placement.

Why are people so fickle about something so fundamental? Mr Claassen reckons that the introduction of certain liberal aspects of democracy – such as the protection of individual rights and checks on executive power – may dampen support for it. These features may be more difficult for the public to accept than principles such as majority rule (which even some authoritarian regimes embrace). The study is a reminder that support for democracy cannot be taken for granted. Although it may be better than any alternative form of government that has been tried from time to time, it is still far from perfect.

Are women less interested in politics than men?

Western society has no shortage of stereotypes about the activities and interests of men and women. Have they shaped how they think about politics? When asked the question "How interested would you say you are in politics?", the share of men who answer "very" or "fairly" interested is significantly larger than that of women. This phenomenon has been observed across more than a dozen rich countries. It may have harmful consequences. If women are less interested in politics, they may be less likely to take part in it, including voting or running for office. And their views – particularly on social issues like workplace equality, parental leave and child care, which they care about on average more than men do – may not be adequately represented in government.

A study by Marta Fraile of the Institute of Public Goods and Policies in Madrid and Irene Sánchez-Vítores of the European University Institute finds that the gap in political interest appears early in life. Using data from the British Household Panel Survey, which polled 10,300 people between 1991 and 2009, the authors

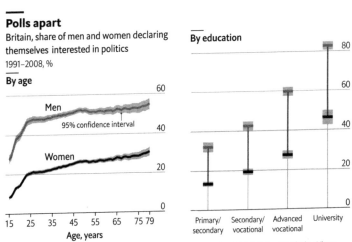

Polls apart

Britain, share of men and women declaring themselves interested in politics
1991–2008, %

By age

By education

Source: "Tracing the gender gap in political interest over the life span: a panel analysis", M. Fraile and I. Sánchez-Vítores, *Political Psychology*, 2019

find that the gender gap among 15-year-old Britons is already about 20 percentage points. For 25-year-olds, it grows to roughly 30 points. For better-educated people, who tend to be more engaged in politics, the divide is even greater. Among British adults with a university degree, the gender gap in interest in politics is a whopping 37 percentage points.

The authors suggest several possible explanations for the gap, ranging from social norms to the under-representation of women in public life. They note one intriguing correlation. In countries with more gender equality – as measured by an index developed by the European Institute for Gender Equality, a think-tank – the gap in interest in politics tends to be smaller. In Portugal, it is about 30 percentage points; but in Denmark and Finland, where women enjoy a comparatively high degree of equality, it is just 10 points.

Why Brittany wants its own emoji

France's foreign minister, Jean-Yves Le Drian, is a man of few words and many air miles. When he does comment, it is usually to deplore events in Syria, say, or Iran. But in February 2020 the minister let his inner passion get the better of him. The reason? An emoji. "The countdown is on!" Mr Le Drian tweeted excitedly. All Bretons, he urged, should mobilise on social media by tweeting a hashtag, as part of a campaign to secure an emoji for the Brittany flag, known as the *Gwenn ha du*. "Go on, tweet our #emojiBZH and don't let up!"

Mr Le Drian, born in the Brittany town of Lorient, was merely the latest to join an effort to turn the black-and-white striped Brittany flag into a digital icon. Promoted by www.bzh (an organisation, not a website), which runs the Breton internet domain name, and the Brittany region, the campaign first stirred interest in 2017. On "world emoji day" that year, to Bretons' delight, the *Gwenn ha du* was voted the second most-wanted emoji worldwide. (It narrowly lost to *mate*, an infusion popular in Latin America.) In January 2020 a fresh effort was made to demonstrate to the Unicode Consortium, a global body that approves new emoji, the extent of popular backing for the Brittany flag. Within hours, the hashtag #emojiBZH was trending at the top of Twitter in France.

Competition for new emoji is fierce. Raclette, an Alpine melted-cheese dish, was rejected as too obscure. The Unicode Consortium says some emoji are unnecessary because they can be approximated by others. A squirrel, it insists, can be represented by a chipmunk emoji. But the same logic cannot be applied to flags. Requests for emoji for the Tibetan and Catalan flags are still pending – although there is one for the Isle of Man, and the French island of La Réunion.

An independent kingdom in the 9th century, Brittany became part of France in 1532. But regional identity has been fiercely defended, with periodic revolts, ever since. Today Breton pride and powerful networks endure. François Pinault, a luxury-goods tycoon who hails from the region, flies the Breton flag from the Venetian palace that houses his art collection. In 2018, when introducing

Mr Le Drian to the pope, President Emmanuel Macron joked that "Bretons are everywhere, it's the French mafia!" Now, though, Mr Macron seems to have swung behind the campaign for the emoji. When his official photographer, a Bretonne, tweeted in its favour, he gave it the presidential "like".

How to predict a coup

Two ageing presidents, one bad and one awful, were forced from office in April 2019: Abdelaziz Bouteflika in Algeria and Omar al-Bashir in Sudan. Mr Bouteflika had been in power since 1999; Mr Bashir, since 1989. Their hasty and unlamented departures raised a question: how easy is it to predict a coup?

Coups and revolutions present unique challenges for forecasters. They are both extremely rare and, notes Andreas Beger of Predictive Heuristics, a consultancy, by definition conspiratorial – they do not advertise themselves in advance. Perhaps the most rigorous quantitative forecast of political upheaval comes from One Earth Future (OEF), an NGO based in Colorado that publishes a predictive model, CoupCast. It reckons that the factors correlating most strongly with the risk of a coup include: the rate of economic growth; how long a regime has been in power; how long it has been since a country's most recent coup; and whether it has been hit by extreme weather, such as a flood or a drought.

Economic woes certainly played a part in the defenestrations of Mr Bouteflika and Mr Bashir. But the relationship between prosperity and political stability is complex. In 2015 a report from the World Bank noted that economic indicators alone could not have predicted the advent of the Arab Spring in 2011. Economies in the Middle East and North Africa were growing steadily. Extreme poverty and income inequality were falling. But despite the rosy headline numbers, surveys conducted in the 2000s found that Arabs were growing increasingly worried about their financial prospects. In Tunisia, where the Arab Spring began, 23% of graduates were unemployed in 2010, compared with only 13% for the population as a whole. This suggests that a lack of opportunities mattered more than poverty.

Political history matters, too. CoupCast finds that both new and very old autocratic regimes are at risk of being overthrown. Emerging tyrants need time to consolidate power. Longer-standing regimes like those of Mr Bouteflika and Mr Bashir tend to fade

Reasons to be careful
Worldwide, factors affecting coups, 2019

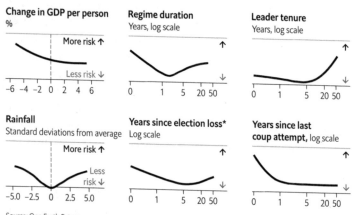

Source: One Earth Future

*For dictators who stay on even after losing

as their leaders age. CoupCast's data find that for dictators, the "sweet spot" in terms of political stability comes very early in their despotism – after just 18 months. Clayton Besaw of the OEF says one way dictators have adapted to modern politics is by choosing to hold elections. This is a risky strategy. Winning elections can help legitimise their regimes, but trying to stay on after losing tends to create further instability.

Which country then, has the highest chance of seeing a sudden regime change? The strongest predictor of future instability is past instability. CoupCast rated Algeria the country most likely to experience a coup just before Mr Bouteflika's exit. As for who might be next, the leaders of Burkina Faso, Afghanistan and South Sudan should be nervous.

Why the Democratic party is symbolised by a donkey

Thomas Nast, a German-born caricaturist, has been hailed as "the father of the American cartoon" by critics and historians. His most famous work appeared in *Harper's Weekly* between 1862 and 1886; at the time *Harper's* was one of America's most popular magazines, with a circulation of around 120,000. His style was dense – meant to be pored over, rather than absorbed at a glance – with lots of minute explanatory labels and an allegorical mode rich in literary and biblical references. Sadly for the Democratic Party, Nast was also a committed Republican. His images were often abrasive, excoriating those he believed were in the wrong. Nast was even referred to as "the president maker". Abraham Lincoln called Nast his best recruiting sergeant during his re-election campaign.

"A Live Jackass Kicking a Dead Lion", his most significant drawing, was published on January 15th 1870. A play on the proverb "A live ass is better than a dead lion", Nast's cartoon carries a different message. The donkey – ears back, hind legs poised to deliver a vicious blow – is labelled "Copperhead papers", a reference to the newspapers sympathetic to a faction of anti-war Democrats popularly known as "Copperheads" (after a venomous snake). The lion – noble in death, its head cupped by one huge paw – is "Hon. E.M. Stanton", the former secretary of war under Lincoln and a Republican grandee. Behind the pair, on a rocky outcrop, an American eagle turns to glare, and in the background massed ranks of flags allude to the recent civil war and the work needed to heal the nation. The clear message is that any Democrats hostile to this Republican hero are vicious, misjudged and borderline traitorous. Their actions, in short, are those of a jackass.

Nast was not the first to link the Democrats and donkeys. In 1828, when Andrew Jackson was running for election, rivals gave him the nickname "the jackass". (Incivility and name-calling in the political sphere are hardly modern innovations.) Jackson embraced the label, using it in his own campaign and proclaiming that the donkey was a symbol of loyalty, determination and the common man. This in effect quashed its use by critics until after his presidency. Nast, however, can be credited with popularising and cementing the association. He used the donkey again and again to represent the Democrats. In "Fine-Ass Committee" (February 1874), a Democratic congressman with a donkey's head blows bubbles of inflation from a cup of soft soap. In March 1876 another ass-headed Democrat pins a sign reading "The New Democratic Slate" onto a snarling Democratic tiger. The party, to Nast, was dangerous and out of control: no reforms and initiatives could change that.

Although Nast was partisan, Republicans did not get off scot-free. The Republican elephant made its lumbering debut in an unflattering cartoon on November 7th 1874, in "The Third-Term Panic". In it, a donkey ("N.Y Herald", a Democratic newspaper) has donned a lion's skin connoting Caesarism, hoping to frighten the other political beasts with tales of Ulysses Grant's supposed desire to run for a third term. Away flee the "N.Y. Times" unicorn, the "N.Y. Tribune" giraffe, the slinking Democratic Party fox and, towering over them all, a pachyderm labelled "The Republican vote". The elephant is so terrified it is in the act of trampling over planks – labelled "Home Rule" and "Reform" – and falling into an abyss. To modern eyes, Nast's cartoons are hard to decode, requiring knowledge of political history. But his use of animals to represent America's two main parties endures to this day.

Why Republicans eat more meat than Democrats

Politics usually comes first on lists of "what not to discuss at Thanksgiving". Under President Donald Trump, the subject has been unusually hard to avoid. One Thanksgiving strategy, you might think, would be to focus on talking about food instead. But be warned: ideas on what people should eat are inextricably linked with politics. One clear example is the ethics of eating meat. Vegetarian and vegan meals abound in upscale American supermarkets. But whereas Democrats may be keen on trying "tofurkey" (provided it is gluten-free), the idea is as repulsive to Republicans as sitting through a marathon of Michael Moore documentaries.

To illustrate just how divided Americans are on their holiday's signature dish, *The Economist* asked YouGov, a polling firm, to survey 1,500 adults in the country in 2019 about their attitudes towards eating meat. Despite the growing abundance of plant-based meat substitutes, only 5% and 2% of Americans identified as vegetarians and vegans, respectively. Much of the demand for quinoa burgers probably comes from omnivores worried about both their own health and the lives of the animals they eat. Twenty-seven per cent of respondents in our survey said they had made an effort to reduce their consumption of meat in the previous year. Here the partisan divide was stark, with 35% of Democrats but only 21% of Republicans trying to cut down.

What explains this difference? Blaming it all on politics would be a mistake. Democrats tend to be younger and better-educated. Democrats are also more likely to be women and live in big cities. All of these traits are correlated with greater apprehensiveness about eating animals. Was it really the political ideology of people who preferred Hillary Clinton to Donald Trump that led them to eat less meat? It seems more likely that Democrats simply belong to demographic groups in which vegetarianism is more common.

Isolating the impact of partisanship on a person's taste for turkey is difficult, since political-party affiliation is strongly correlated

Don't have a cow, man

Americans who say they have made an effort to reduce their
consumption of meat over the past year*, %

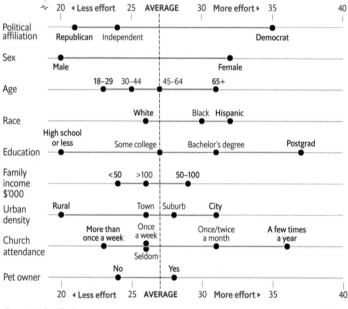

Sources: YouGov; *The Economist*   *Survey November 2018

with many demographic variables. We tried to separate out its effect
using a logistic regression model, which estimated the probability
that a survey respondent would say they had tried to reduce their
meat consumption based on their political-party preference, sex,
age, ethnicity, education, household income, whether they live
in a city or a rural area, how often they go to church and whether
they own any pets. Our study found that even after introducing all
of these controls, Democrats were still about 1.8 times as likely as
Republicans to say they wanted to reduce their meat consumption.
That suggests that the safest course of action at a Thanksgiving
dinner may be to sit and eat in silence.

How medieval Catholicism nudged Europe towards democracy

Why some countries are rich and others are poor is an enduring debate in economics. Natural resources and friendly climates help only a bit. In contrast, robust political institutions and a steady rule of law seem essential. But why did these precursors evolve in just a few dozen states? One oft-cited theory, advanced by Robert Putnam of Harvard University, is that the crucial ingredient is "social capital", the affinity people feel for members of their society whom they do not know. Proxies for this sentiment, such as blood-donation rates or propensity to return a stranger's lost wallet, closely track GDP per person. Social capital can take centuries to amass. Mr Putnam has shown that parts of Italy that were ruled by a feudal monarchy around 1300AD have low levels of social trust and are relatively poor today. In contrast, the Italian regions that formed city-states in that era, where citizens banded together for commerce and self-defence, are now unusually rich and well run.

A study by Jonathan Schulz, Joseph Henrich and colleagues proposes an explanation that delves even further back in time. They focus on family structure. Until recent human history, people lived in small groups and often married relatives. These habits reinforced family ties, but made people wary of outsiders. In Europe this started to change around 500AD, when the Catholic church began banning polygamy and marriages between cousins, or between widows or widowers and their dead spouses' siblings. These edicts forced unmarried men to venture out and meet women from different social groups. The paper says that this reduced Christians' "conformity and in-group loyalty", and made them trust strangers more. By expanding the community beyond clans, it helped create the broad solidarity on which development may depend.

To show that Christian dogma caused this shift, the authors match historical data on the spread of religion with modern indicators. In places where Catholicism was generally the leading religion from 500AD to 1500AD, people score highly on measures of independence, impartiality and trust – such as agreeing to testify against a friend whose reckless driving killed a pedestrian. The same pattern occurs in countries settled mostly by Christian migrants, such as the United States and Canada. In contrast, social trust is lower and marriage between cousins is relatively common in areas whose populations do not descend from medieval Catholics.

This effect distinguishes Catholicism from other strands of medieval Christianity. Years spent before 1500AD under Eastern Orthodoxy, which the authors say did less to police marriage within families, was a weaker predictor of "pro-social" survey responses than exposure to Catholicism was. Moreover, the trend holds up both between and within countries. Among Italian regions, those with high social capital (as measured by data like using cheques over cash) were influenced by Catholicism for longer than those lacking it were. The study's subject limits the strength of its findings. Barring an experiment to assign religions to countries at random and monitor them for 1,500 years, no one can prove whether incest bans built social trust or merely coincided with it. Nonetheless, the paper bolsters the case for studying history to understand the present.

Transports of delight: travel and tourism

Charting the decline in legroom on planes

"You can curl up in the big roomy seat... or if you're a six-footer, you can stretch out to your long legs' content!" So promised a 1960s-era advert for United Airlines, then America's biggest carrier. Today, most passengers can only dream of such luxury. Aeroplane seats have become ever more cramped – and they are not about to get roomier.

In the 1960s, passengers could indeed stretch out at 35,000 feet. Back then the distance between rows – known as seat pitch – was around 35 inches in economy class. But after America deregulated air travel in 1978, ticket prices dropped, and legroom and seat width soon followed. In the past two decades, as airlines have crammed ever more seats onto their planes, the average width of an airline seat has narrowed from 18.5 to 17 inches. Seat pitch has shrunk from 35 to about 31 inches, according to Flyers' Rights, an advocacy group.

Some airlines are roomier than others. JetBlue, Japan Air and Turkish Airlines all boast an economy-class pitch of 33–34 inches; Alaska Airlines, Southwest and Emirates give passengers 32 inches. Budget airlines, unsurprisingly, offer the least space: easyJet and Ryanair, Europe's two largest low-cost carriers, provide just 30 inches; Spirit Airlines, an American discount carrier, offers a paltry 28.

Cost-conscious flyers are rarely satisfied with their cramped quarters. Naturally, airlines have responded by offering them a little extra space – for a price. Seats once considered standard size are now sold as "premium economy". Seats in exit rows, which need a bigger pitch to accommodate emergency-exit doors, cost more on many routes. First-class passengers, meanwhile, can luxuriate in up to 90 inches of space, while business-class travellers enjoy up to 82 inches.

Many rage against the squeezing of the flight, to little end. In Asia, where 100m people fly for the first time every year, carriers have been determined to squeeze in passengers anywhere they can. Cebu Air, in the Philippines, even promised to move kitchens

Pitch perfect
Distribution of airline-seat pitch* by ticket class, inches
December 2019

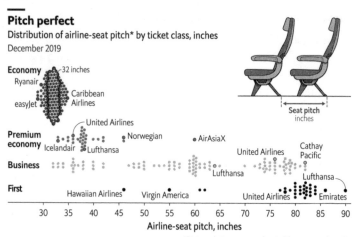

Source: Skytrax

*Distance between a row of seats. Measurement from the same position on two seats, one behind the other

and bathrooms to do so. In 2018 America's Federal Aviation Administration (FAA) said it would not regulate airline-seat size, despite concerns that it is hard to evacuate planes into which more and more passengers are crammed. Even narrow seats with puny pitches, the FAA argued, allow passengers to get out safely. It declared: "The FAA has no evidence that a typical passenger, even a larger one, will take more than a couple of seconds to get out of his or her seat."

How much should you tip an Uber driver?

Working out how much to tip in America is never easy. Bartenders, it is said, should be tipped $1 a drink, the equivalent of 10% for a $10 cocktail. Waiters, meanwhile, apparently deserve 15–20%. Such questions of tipping etiquette are baffling, and it is hard to know whether you are being more or less generous than average. But there is at least one industry in which the practice is becoming less mysterious, allowing customers to calibrate their tipping more precisely if they wish to do so. A paper by four economists, Bharat Chandar, Uri Gneezy, John A. List and Ian Muir, analyses more than 40m Uber trips taken in 2017 across America to understand just how much ride-hailing customers tip their drivers.

Whether a taxi ride ends with a tip, it turns out, depends far more on the passenger than the person behind the wheel. The authors found that nearly 60% of people never tip; 1% always do so. Men are more likely to tip than women (17% v 14%) and give more generously ($3.13 v $3.07 on average). Uber passengers rated five stars by drivers, based on previous trips, are more than twice as likely to tip as those with just 4.75 stars. When they tip, they give nearly 14% more.

Savvy drivers can therefore boost their earnings if they know whom to pick up. They have less control, however, over other factors. Female drivers, who account for just one in six trips, earn more in tips, on average, than their male counterparts (12% more from male customers and 11% from female ones), particularly if they are young. A woman aged 21 to 25 can expect to earn four cents more on each trip than a similarly aged man. By age 65 this tip premium – relative to a 20-something man – disappears.

This does not mean that a driver's performance on the road is immaterial. "Hard accelerations" reduce a driver's tip by an average of 0.7 cents. "Hard brakes" reduce tips by 1.3 cents, on average. One might think that speedier drivers, able to get their passengers to the airport or train station on time, would be rewarded for their efforts. In fact, "speeding episodes" reduce tips by an average of 2.9 cents.

Tipping points

United States, tipping habits of Uber passengers, Aug–Sep 2017

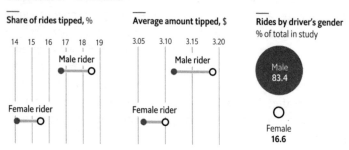

Source: "The drivers of social preferences: evidence from a nationwide tipping field experiment",
B. Chandar *et al.*, National Bureau of Economic Research, 2019

So if you are a rider who wishes to prioritise speed over comfort, it is worth telling your driver – and then tipping generously when you reach your destination.

How to protect airliners from missiles

The shooting-down of Ukraine International Airlines flight 752 over Iran on January 8th 2020, killing 176 people, provoked outrage around the world – not least in Iran, where it triggered a new round of anti-government protests. Mixed with the grief and anger was disbelief that an international airline was willing – and allowed – to fly through a potential conflict zone. Iran inexplicably failed to close its airspace to civilian airliners even though it was on alert for retaliation after firing ballistic missiles at American forces in Iraq, and had deployed anti-aircraft systems near its main international airport.

Such catastrophes are rare, but not as rare as they should be. In 1983 a Soviet fighter jet shot down a Korean Air plane that had strayed into Soviet airspace at the same time as an American reconnaissance craft. Five years later the USS *Vincennes*, an American cruiser, mistook an Iranian airliner for an incoming warplane and shot it down, killing 290 passengers and crew. In 2001, during a military exercise, Ukraine's armed forces mistakenly shot down a Russian airliner returning home from Israel, killing 78 people. In 2014 Russian-backed separatists shot down Malaysia Airlines flight 17 (MH17) over eastern Ukraine, killing 298 people.

What can be done to protect airliners, whether from attacks by terrorists, carelessness or accidents in the fog of war? One step is to improve perimeter security around airports. Under normal conditions, incoming and departing aircraft fly low enough to be hit by a shoulder-fired missile (below around 6,000 metres or 20,000 feet) for about 40km. That creates a zone of vulnerability of nearly 800 square kilometres. So a second step, often used in conflict zones, is for pilots to adapt their flying techniques to reduce the risk. Corkscrew landings and steep climb-outs bring passengers to safety as quickly as possible. A third approach is to use on-board defence systems. In 2002 al-Qaeda terrorists in Kenya fired two surface-to-air missiles at a plane operated by El Al, Israel's flag-carrier, narrowly missing it. Afterwards El Al equipped its fleet with missile-defence systems – decoy flares and lasers to disrupt heat-seeking missiles. (This was expensive, but was paid for by government subsidies.) The best protection is avoidance. At cruising altitude, airliners fly beyond the reach of the man-portable missile systems that terrorists are most likely to obtain. But they are still within the range of vehicle-mounted weapons such as the Buk and Tor systems that struck the Malaysian plane in 2014 and the Ukrainian one in 2020. Normally these are only available to national armies (Russia had provided the Buk to Ukrainian separatists). Passenger jets broadcast information to identify themselves as civilian airliners rather than military aircraft, but errors can happen all too easily.

Sharing information could help, too. Sovereign states have sole legal responsibility for ensuring the safety of their airspace. But many are reluctant to admit to dangers that might tarnish their image or threaten revenues from overflight permits. National aviation regulators can ban their airlines from flying through another country's airspace if they deem it to be dangerous. But different regulators often have different assessments of risk, and airlines may be reluctant to incur the costs of cancellations and detours. Many of these weaknesses were tragically apparent in Tehran in January 2020. One problem is that intelligence about potential threats is not always shared between governments, regulators and airlines, nor acted upon if it is. After the attack on MH17, the International Civil Aviation Organisation, a UN agency, created a website where countries could report threats relating to their airspace and that of other countries. It was nixed after just two years because it was hardly used.

The paradox of Britain's buses

Never mind the snazzy, expensive HS2 railway line that the government grudgingly approved on February 11th 2020. What really stirs politicians' hearts is the humble bus. Both the former chancellor of the exchequer, Sajid Javid, and the mayor of London, Sadiq Khan, are the sons of bus drivers, as they are not shy of saying. Boris Johnson, the prime minister, claims to love buses so much that he models them out of wine crates. Alongside the HS2 announcement he promised to throw more money at them. That was a canny move. Buses account for more public-transport trips than trains, tubes and trams put together. People love them, in theory: one poll by Transport Focus, a consumer group, found that 74% of young people think they are a good way of getting around and 85% believe it is important for a place to have a good bus service. There is just one problem: in practice, Britons are taking buses less and less. Powerful forces are driving this trend – probably too powerful to be counteracted with a dollop of public money.

Until recently, the decline in bus use could be put down to bad policies and austerity. In 1986, with Margaret Thatcher in her pomp, bus transport outside London was privatised and deregulated. Bus companies piled in to the best routes; the less popular ones were neglected, especially after the financial crisis, when subsidies were cut. Fares have risen, which deters more people from taking the bus. "It's a cycle of decline," says Darren Shirley of the Campaign for Better Transport. But if deregulation, service cuts and higher fares are the problem, why were London buses emptier in 2019 than in 2015? They have suffered none of those things. Yet the decades-long rise in bus trips in the capital – which was driven by good management, subsidies, a booming economy, rapid population growth, ever more unpleasant driving conditions and costly parking – appears to have reversed. Something else is up.

One thing that has changed is young people's behaviour. The young are heavy bus users when they travel. But, increasingly, they do not travel. According to Transport for London, the average 17- to

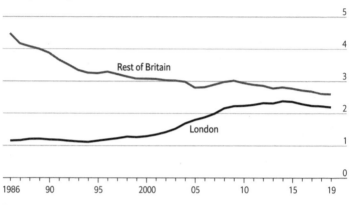

Move down, please
Passenger journeys on local bus services, bn

Source: Department for Transport

24-year-old took 2.3 transport trips per day in the fiscal year 2011–12 but only 1.7 in 2018–19. The National Travel Survey confirms that no group has cut back harder on travel since the early 2000s than teenagers. Young people are more diligent these days, and stay in school for longer. They can do the things that young people love to do – flirting, joking and playing with their friends – on their phones, without going out.

The other big bus users are the poor (who have few other options) and the old (who can travel for nothing). Especially outside London, both are shunning buses for cars. Since 2002 the proportion of households in the poorest quintile who have no car has fallen a bit, from 49% to 46%. The fall among the second-poorest quintile is sharper: 36% to 28%. Relaxed lending standards have made cars easier to acquire; frugal engines make them cheaper to run. Cars are ever more comfortable and idiot-proof, with parking-assist technology and lane-drifting alerts to help doddery drivers. Outside London, the average free bus-pass was used 90 times in the fiscal year 2010–11 but only 74 times in 2018–19, according to the Department for Transport.

Finally, there is the gig economy. Online shopping and Uber probably substitute for bus trips as well as private-car journeys. And they put new vehicles on the roads, which slows everything down. The number of light-goods vehicles in London has risen by 28% since 2012. Tony Travers of the London School of Economics points out that bus speeds have fallen slightly in the capital, even though private cars have almost been purged from the city centre. The average London bus now travels at 9.3 miles per hour. Just as people become less inclined to run after buses, they are becoming easier to catch.

Why Airbus stopped making the A380 super-jumbo

After a century of refining their craft, planemakers have become masters of building safe, reliable jets that bring air travel within reach of the masses. Occasionally their products win cult status among passengers. Concorde, the world's only reliable supersonic passenger jet, wowed travellers for nearly three decades. But it was a financial disaster that only stayed airborne because of vast government subsidies. Sixteen years after Concorde's final flight in 2003, another aircraft that passengers love to fly has also been given the chop: the A380. Its maker, Airbus, announced in February 2019 that it would cease production of the super-jumbo by 2021.

The A380 is the biggest passenger plane ever built. It can carry nearly 900 people, though airlines tend to fill it with about 500 seats. Its spacious cabins, smooth take-offs and quiet engines were an instant hit when the plane took to the skies in 2007. At 580 tonnes when fully loaded, the A380 is a flying hippopotamus that seems to be too large, and move too slowly, to stay aloft; a testament to the supremacy of science over intuition, beauty and – unfortunately – economics. Perhaps the only people who are not enchanted by the A380 are the accountants tasked with finding routes on which it can make money. Airbus conceived the double-decker as a solution to a growing shortage of runway capacity at busy airports. When filled to capacity, the aircraft offers lower ticket prices than any other long-haul plane. But the task of filling it every day is tough. Only the world's very biggest carriers had enough scale to consider buying such an aircraft, and too few of them took the plunge. Sales numbered in the low hundreds instead of the thousands once expected.

The A380's biggest backer was Emirates, the flag-carrier of Dubai. It was responsible for more than half of the 321 units sold. But the airline has run out of room for expansion at its hub in Dubai International Airport. Moreover, smaller, more fuel-efficient planes, such as Boeing's 787, can make non-stop flights cheaply between

Europe and Asia competitive, sapping demand for connecting flights via the Middle East. Emirates has responded by slowing its plans for growth. In February 2019 it reduced an order for 53 super-jumbos to just 14, ordering smaller A330 and A350 planes instead. Qantas, Australia's flag-carrier, also cancelled its remaining orders for the super-jumbo. These announcements precipitated Airbus's decision to stop making it.

Meanwhile, once-loyal operators such as Singapore Airlines and Air France are starting to get rid of the planes. Some of the first A380s that Airbus built are even being scrapped: early models consumed too much fuel and were too expensive to insure to continue to be used profitably. But other A380s could have happier retirements. Leasing firms that operate flights on behalf of other carriers, to provide extra capacity at peak times, are interested in buying them. So the A380 will continue to lumber implausibly across the skies for some years yet.

The case for weighing passengers before flights

A favourite pastime of air passengers is to moan about all the extra fees that airlines have introduced in recent years. First came charges for stowing baggage in the hold, then more for in-flight food, allocated seating and even for using the overhead lockers. Would the idea to charge passengers according to their weight be a fee too far? That is exactly what would be done under a proposal from Fuel Matrix, a British firm: to weigh passengers before they board a flight. The company has held talks with several airports about "discreet" ways to introduce weighing technology. According to the company's chief executive, Roy Fuscone, flyers' weights will be stored in the same secure system as facial-recognition data, another technology some airports are trying out to eliminate the need for paper tickets at boarding gates.

The scheme would probably go down very badly with flyers. Some would see it as a cynical means of charging larger passengers extra. And it would grate culturally in parts of the world where "fat shaming" is socially unacceptable. Yet weighing passengers used to be the norm, particularly in the early days of aviation. Before the second world war, most passengers in America and Europe were weighed before take-off and charged more for extra heft. This was because early planes were smaller and had strict weight limits. For instance, on the inaugural flight of the Boeing 247 airliner in 1933, from San Francisco to New York, the plane could not carry more than 16,805 pounds (7,621kg) including fuel. So the ten passengers with tickets had to get on the scales, as did the flight attendant, who could not weigh more than 135 pounds.

The practice was phased out as airlines began to rely on broad guidelines to estimate how much passengers weighed. But to be on the safe side, this requires airlines to carry more fuel than they need to for each passenger. Airline executives reckon that carrying all that extra unnecessary kerosene around further increases fuel consumption. That not only pushes up the cost of tickets, but also means that more emissions are produced than is needed. Hence the temptation for airlines to weigh passengers again – and some have started to do so.

In 2013 Samoa Air attracted international attention when it began charging passengers according to their weight (it went bust two years later). In 2015 Uzbekistan Airways started measuring how heavy flyers were for safety reasons. But predictably, the practice has drawn criticism from passengers. In 2016 Hawaiian Airlines announced that it would assign seats on flights to American Samoa based on passengers' weights, to ensure even distribution. Samoans, who have one of the world's highest rates of obesity, said this policy was racially discriminatory. They filed complaints with American regulators, who ultimately sided with the airline. But the bad publicity will not have escaped the notice of other airlines. Michael O'Leary of Ryanair, Europe's biggest low-cost carrier, who has pioneered charging passengers extra for all sorts of things, raised the possibility of imposing weight surcharges a decade ago. But not even he has dared to try it.

Why Hong Kong's airport was a good target for protesters

The musical adaptation of *Les Misérables*, Victor Hugo's novel about the failed revolutionaries of mid-19th-century France, is probably the most successful theatrical production of the neo-liberal age. The English-language version, which ran in London from 1985 until 2019, was the longest-running musical in the West End, and the second longest-running in the world. Its best-known song – "Do You Hear The People Sing?" – can be heard at protest marches around the world. It was sung (in Cantonese) several times inside the terminal of Hong Kong International Airport during the protests that began in mid-2019. There are some similarities between the Hong Kong protests and those depicted in *Les Misérables*. Both groups are inspired by liberal values, rather than the socialism or communism more commonly associated with the revolutions of the 20th century. And just like the narrow streets of Paris, the airport's terminals were a very good place to hold a protest.

The revolutionaries of *Les Misérables* found it easy to build barricades across narrow streets with household furniture and goods, turning neighbourhoods into mini-fortresses. Paris's revolution of 1830 saw over 4,000 barricades put up across the city; in that of 1848 there were at least 6,000. They proved such a menace that Emperor Napoleon III had the medieval streets swept away in Europe's biggest redevelopment project, led by Baron Haussmann, who replaced them with wide boulevards. These made Paris indefensible from Prussian cavalry in 1870 and German tanks in 1940.

Hong Kong's main airport terminal, designed by Norman Foster, a hugely influential contemporary architect, has its own attractive qualities for protesters. As the city's only airport, it could quickly cripple transport links to the rest of the world, ensuring that any protest would quickly gain international media coverage. It also has good public transport connections to move protesters quickly in and out. The most famous bits of Mr Foster's design are its glass walls, open departure halls and narrow glass walkways over deep atriums. The walkways could easily be blocked by improvised barricades made from baggage trolleys. The glass walls and open spaces meant the police were less able to use violence without being caught on camera.

The airport is not the only building designed by Mr Foster to have housed protests. Its design was inspired by that of Stansted Airport, built in Britain earlier in the 1990s. He also used the same philosophy in a building for Cambridge University's Faculty of Law, which looks so similar to an airport terminal that students joke he got the plans mixed up with those for Stansted. In 2009, the Faculty of Law building was the target of a sit-in protest about humanitarian relief for Palestinians. Students chose the building for very similar reasons to protesters in Hong Kong. The walls are transparent, offering good views to any student journalists. And the building has only one usable entrance and staircase, with access to each floor along relatively narrow walkways. So a protest blockading the lobby and walkways could shut it down very quickly.

Yet the fate of the revolutionaries in *Les Misérables*, and the protesters in the Faculty of Law hold a lesson for those in Hong Kong. Most of the revolutionaries on the Parisian barricades have been shot dead by the time the curtain falls in *Les Misérables*. The protest in Cambridge's Law Faculty was the longest-lasting protest of its kind at any British university in 2009, but was also the only one that ended with the university authorities refusing to cave in to any of the protesters' demands to help the Palestinian cause. Hong Kong airport's architecture may suit a protest or a revolution well. But that does not necessarily give it any greater chance of success.

Why seaplanes are so dangerous

On May 13th 2019 the pilot of a seaplane flying over Alaska steered to give a better view of a waterfall, just as he had done on many flights before. This time, he saw a flash on his left – and crashed into another plane. Both aircraft plunged into the sea, killing six people. The following week another seaplane crashed in Alaska with two more fatalities. America's National Transportation Safety Board (NTSB), the government agency that investigates such accidents, warned that seaplanes, which are able to take off and land on water, may no longer be a safe form of transport. It asked the Federal Aviation Administration, a regulator, to upgrade its rules about seaplanes, which currently fall far short of safety regulations for other commercial aircraft.

Seaplanes used to be the main form of air transport before the second world war, during which America and Europe were carpeted, for military reasons, with concrete runways suitable for large passenger jets. But it is not just weaker regulation that makes these sorts of planes dangerous today. The lack of a runway on solid ground is also a problem – one of the reasons seaplanes fell out of favour seven decades ago. The most exhaustive study of seaplane accidents on water, published by the Canadian government in 1994, found that over two-thirds of fatalities were caused by drowning, rather than the crash impact itself. As the report noted, "had these accidents occurred on land, a large percentage of them might have been non-fatal". This is because it is difficult to safely evacuate a seaplane on water. The report found that only 8% of occupants of these planes were able to escape easily, against 26% who escaped with difficulty. Nearly half did not escape at all. The same report found that only 0.2% of nose-over or nose-down accidents on take-off or landing were fatal for land-based aircraft, compared with 10% for seaplanes.

There are several reasons for this. Seaplanes often flip upside down during a crash landing, which is relatively rare on land. Passengers who are scared of jumping into the water can block escape routes. For those who do escape, help takes longer to organise and arrive than on land. And icy water, which can cause hypothermia, can kill otherwise unharmed passengers. Pressure to fly seaplanes in less than ideal weather is also a problem. They are often chartered by cruise lines, particularly in Alaska, as a quick way to give passengers a tour of the landscape. But cruise lines want these flights to start and end on time so their passengers do not delay the ship setting sail. As a result, the NTSB has found, some seaplane pilots feel pressured by tight cruise-ship schedules to carry out excursions even when conditions are dangerous.

Despite all this, any attempt at a regulatory crackdown on seaplanes in America seems likely to run into political resistance. Alaska is particularly reliant on them. Most of the state is inaccessible by road and the tourism industry there is heavily reliant on seaplanes to get visitors around. Alaskans are also six times more likely than the average American to own a plane. Seaplanes may have fallen from favour, but they are likely to be around for some time yet.

Estonia's new way to punish speeding motorists

Time is money. That, at least, is the principle behind an innovative scheme being tested in Estonia to deal with dangerous driving. During trials that began in 2019, anyone caught speeding along the road between Tallinn and the town of Rapla was stopped and given a choice. They could pay a fine, as usual, or take a "timeout" instead – waiting for 45 minutes or an hour, depending on how fast they were going when stopped. In other words, they could pay the fine in time rather than money.

The aim of the experiment was to see how drivers perceive speeding, and whether loss of time might be a stronger deterrent than loss of money. The project is a collaboration between Estonia's Home Office and the police force, and is part of a programme designed to encourage innovation in public services. Government teams propose a problem they would like to solve – such as traffic accidents caused by irresponsible driving – and work under the guidance of an innovation unit. Teams are expected to do all fieldwork and interviews themselves.

"At first it was kind of a joke," says Laura Aaben, an innovation adviser for the interior ministry, referring to the idea of timeouts. "But we kept coming back to it." Elari Kasemets, Ms Aaben's counterpart in the police force, explains that, in interviews, drivers frequently said that having to spend time dealing with the police and being given a speeding ticket was more annoying than the cost of the ticket itself. "People pay the fines, like bills, and forget about it," he says. (In Estonia, speeding fines generated by automatic cameras are not kept on record and have no cumulative effect, meaning that drivers do not have their licences revoked if they get too many.)

Making drivers wait imposes costs on the police, because it requires manpower. The team acknowledges that the experiment cannot currently be scaled up, but hopes that technology could solve that problem in the future. Public reaction, though, was not what the team expected. "It's been very positive, surprisingly," says Helelyn Tammsaar, who manages projects for the innovation unit. Estonians have praised the idea for being more egalitarian: monetary fines are not adjusted according to income, as they are in neighbouring Finland, because everyone has the same number of hours in the day. They also perceive the punishment as a reasonable punishment for the offence, rather than a means of filling state coffers.

The life-saving effect of painting lines on roads

Fifteen minutes into Alfred Hitchcock's film *North by Northwest*, Roger Thornhill, the character played by Cary Grant, already has a heap of problems. Having been mistaken for another man, he has been kidnapped by two armed thugs and driven out of New York City. The thugs have poured a large bourbon into him and put him behind the wheel of a car, which they have aimed over the edge of a cliff. Thornhill has another problem, which heightens the drama. The road's edge is unmarked.

When *North by Northwest* was released, in 1959, most American roads lacked painted edge lines. Even the centre lines shown in that film were not yet standardised.

Did the simple act of painting lines on roads save hundreds of thousands of lives? In their book *Reducing Global Road Traffic Tragedies*, Gerald Balcar and Bo Elfving argue that it did. The first American centre line appeared near Detroit in 1911; the man responsible for it claimed a leaky milk van leaving a white streak inspired him. Over the next few decades, road engineers began to favour yellow centre lines, which were made reflective by adding glass beads to paint. But edge lines remained rare outside cities.

What changed that were studies from the 1950s showing that painted edge lines cut road accidents, especially fatal ones. In the early 1970s Potters Industries (which made the glass beads, and employed Mr Balcar) calculated that driving on a rural road at night was six times deadlier than driving on an urban road during the day. Cars were running off the roads largely because drivers could not see their edges. As edge lines and marked intersections proliferated, and Americans began wearing seat-belts, the road-death rate began to fall. The car chase in the 1968 film *Bullitt* takes place on impeccably engineered roads, with centre lines and edge lines, energy-absorbing crash barriers and soft, obstacle-free road margins. To make such roads deadly, you need muscle cars, insane speeds, a shotgun and a strategically placed petrol station.

Who owns the Northwest Passage?

Mike Pompeo, America's secretary of state, raised Canadian hackles in May 2019 when he said during a speech in Finland that Canada's claim to the Northwest Passage was "illegitimate". He was there to attend the Arctic Council, a body set up by the eight countries around the Arctic Ocean to resolve differences and disputes relating to the polar region. But if Canada does not own the Northwest Passage, who does?

For centuries, finding a route between the Atlantic and the Pacific through the labyrinth of 36,000 islands that form Canada's Arctic archipelago was the dream of ambitious adventurers. Sir John Franklin, a British naval officer, famously perished with his entire crew in 1847 while searching for it. (His expedition's ships, *Erebus* and *Terror*, were only found in 2014 and 2016.) Roald Amundsen, a Norwegian explorer, completed the first successful navigation of the passage in 1906. Since then, global warming has reduced ice coverage in the late summer and early autumn – by more than 30% since 1979, allowing more vessels to operate in the north. Only a few Arctic transits are made each year, mostly on the Russian side of the Arctic Ocean, where there is less ice. Along the Northwest Passage, 289 transits have taken place since 1906, 32 of them in 2017.

America has long maintained that the Northwest Passage, which has up to seven different routes, is an international strait through which its commercial and military vessels have the right to pass without seeking Canada's permission. It bases this claim on the case of the Corfu Channel, separating Albania's coast from the Greek island of Corfu, which was brought before the International Court of Justice in 1947. The court ruled that Albania could not claim the channel as territorial waters because it was an international route for ships between two parts of the high seas over which no country had a claim. Similar disputes exist about the Strait of Hormuz between Iran and Oman; the Bab al-Mandab strait between Yemen and Djibouti; and parts of the South China Sea. Canada, which officially acquired the Arctic archipelago along with

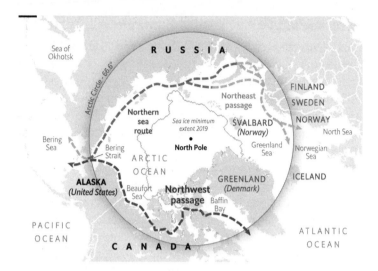

Britain's remaining possessions in North America in 1880, claims sovereignty over the passage because all of its routes run between islands that are Canadian territory. But it has never sought to settle the question in court.

Canada and the United States finessed their disagreement in 1988 with a political rather than a legal fix, called the Arctic Cooperation Agreement. America said it would seek Canada's consent for any transit, but maintained that this did not mean it agreed with Canada's position. Mr Pompeo's comment suggested that, with the Arctic opening up to more shipping, America is no longer happy with the deal. Cargo ships can chop days, if not weeks, off certain journeys by using the Northwest Passage. In 2014 the *Nunavik* took 26 days to carry nickel from Quebec to China, compared with a previous trip through the Panama Canal that took 41 days. But the dispute, like Arctic ice, could be transitory. Scientists now speculate that the entire Arctic Ocean will be ice-free in summer within the next few decades. That means ship owners will not have to ask anyone's permission if they chart a course through the unclaimed high seas at the top of the world.

Why the world's first robot hotel was a disaster

A traveller enters a hotel. She does not see any people behind the reception desk. Instead, a robot takes her name, checks her in, and hands over her room key. Another robot takes her suitcase and escorts her to her room, which has just been cleaned by yet another robot. Is this the future of hospitality? Many pundits have suggested so in recent years, as the cost of robots falls compared with that of hiring staff. But events in Japan suggest otherwise. The world's first robot-operated hotel opened there in 2015. But only four years later, it ended up replacing many of its robots with humans.

The Henn na Hotel ("Strange Hotel") got a slew of publicity and an entry in *Guinness World Records* as the first robot hotel when it opened. It was not just futuristic: its owners hoped to compensate for labour shortages by employing robots to store luggage, mix cocktails, clean rooms and even dance in the lobby. "In countries that suffer from a decreasing population, we think there is a future in robot hotels," said Ayako Matsuo of Huis Ten Bosch, the company that runs the hotel. She claimed that the reduction in labour costs could make robots a "superior" option for hotel staffing.

But when the robots were put in place, things went wrong. The concierge struggled to answer guests' questions. The dancers in the lobby broke down. The luggage-carriers could not climb stairs or go outside. A question-and-answer robot could not handle anything beyond basic inquiries – and responded to at least one guest's snoring by waking him repeatedly to tell him it could not understand what he was saying. Rather than saving labour, the robots actually required the hotel to increase staffing in order to assist and repair the struggling robots. Hence the hotel's decision, in 2019, to lay off more than half of its 243 robots.

Elsewhere in the travel industry, however, the general direction of travel is towards greater automation. For instance, Gatwick Airport near London has been evaluating a robot that will automatically park and retrieve the cars of those flying from its terminals, following similar trials in France and Germany. More hotels are installing automated check-in machines to cut queues in the lobby. In the hotel world, Ms Matsuo believes the future remains a robotic one. The lesson she learned from the struggles at the Henn na Hotel is not that robots were a mistake. Instead, she says, it is that "it is important to separate the services performed by robots and the services performed by humans". Robots, she notes, might not yet be able to anticipate guests' demands in the way that human employees can, but they have abilities that humans lack. Guests come from all over the world, and even the best-educated workforce cannot respond to customers in dozens of languages. Robots may not be staffing hotels by themselves in the imminent future, but their importance in the hospitality industry will surely grow.

Gender agenda: love, sex and marriage

How men and women disagree on what constitutes sexual harassment

The *New York Times* and the *New Yorker* first reported allegations of sexual harassment against Harvey Weinstein in October 2017, sparking the #MeToo movement. In March 2020 the disgraced film producer was sentenced to 23 years in prison for rape and criminal sexual assault. More widely, the case has prompted a global reckoning over sexual abuse by powerful men. But have views on the treatment of women changed in the wake of #MeToo? In October 2017 *The Economist* commissioned YouGov, a pollster, to survey 1,500 American adults about their attitudes towards sexual harassment. Respondents were asked whether 12 different acts – from "asking for a drink" to "requesting a sexual favour" – constituted harassment. The exercise was repeated in October 2018 and again in 2019.

The results suggest that there is just as much disagreement about the boundaries of acceptable behaviour as there was before Mr Weinstein's fall. On the one hand, men seem slightly more aware of the problem: since 2018 the share of male respondents saying the acts covered in our survey qualify as harassment has jumped by nearly five percentage points, on average. On the other hand, the divide between men and women observed in our survey in 2017 remains unchanged, at around five percentage points (which is beyond the margin of error of plus-or-minus two points). This average encompasses much variation: there is little difference between the sexes over asking a woman out for a drink (mostly OK) or flashing (almost never OK). There are more marked differences when it comes to other acts, for example making sexual jokes or grinding in a club. The most striking disagreement concerns looking at a woman's breasts, on which the gap is 24 points.

Disagreement over what is acceptable does not only divide men and women. There is also a split along educational lines. For example, 82% of college-educated men think sexual jokes constitute sexual harassment, whereas only 69% of men without

In the eye of the beholder

"Which of the following would you consider to be sexual harassment?"
By sex of person surveyed, %

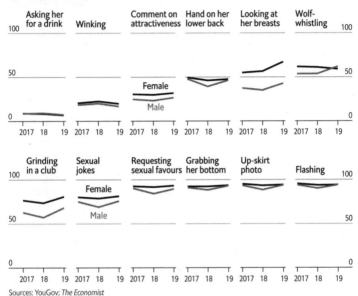

Sources: YouGov; *The Economist*

a college degree think the same. For wolf-whistling, the impact of education levels is striking, even between the two sexes: 71% of college-educated men say that it constitutes harassment; but only 53% of women without a college degree feel the same way.

In Mr Weinstein's case, the verdict on his criminal behaviour is clear. But the rules of everyday behaviour remain much less so. Judging by our survey's findings, society will be arguing over them for years to come.

Scientific papers with male authors are more self-promoting

"Lean In", advises Sheryl Sandberg, Facebook's chief operating officer, in a book of that name. Her advice to women – be more assertive to grab influence at work, rather than waiting for it to be offered – was met with scorn by some feminists. They say that women are not shying away from the higher rungs of the career ladder. Rather, they are being pushed off by unfair forces in the job market, or running into structural barriers as they climb.

A paper published in December 2019 in the *BMJ*, a medical-research journal, offers some support for the idea that men promote themselves more, and that this helps their careers. Marc Lerchenmueller and Olav Sorenson, affiliated with Yale Business School, and Anupam Jena, of Harvard Medical School, examined the language of the titles and abstracts of more than 100,000 clinical-research articles. They separated those in which both the first- and the last-named authors were women from ones in which one or both were men. (The first name in a paper's list of authors is often that of a more junior researcher who led the work, while the last name is usually that of a senior scholar who helped guide it.) Sure enough, articles for which a man was listed as either first or last author were more likely to describe their work in positive terms.

"Novel" was the most commonly self-applied positive term, and those papers with a male first or last author used the word 59.2% more than "women-women" papers with women as both first and last authors. But "promising" was even more skewed: papers with a male first or last author used this word 72.3% more than women-women papers. The researchers further found that such self-promotion was associated with a greater number of subsequent citations, and both effects were bigger in prestigious journals. One possibility is that men really do perform more "novel" and "promising" research than women, and thus merit their self-praise. The paper's authors tried to test this hypothesis by looking at the prestige-rankings of the journals involved, and by comparing similar papers in particular research areas as carefully as possible. Although it is hard to exclude the possibility entirely, other research suggests that men are simply more into self-puffery than women are. They are, for example, more likely to cite themselves, according to an article published in 2017 in *Socius*, a sociology journal.

So should women blow their own trumpets harder? Another paper rebuts that easy conclusion. In a study of economics research, women were subject to more comments from reviewers, and made to revise their submissions more. Women's "readability scores" (a measure rewarding short words and sentences) increased over subsequent drafts, and over subsequent papers across their careers, while men's did not. In trying to please stubborn reviewers, women seem to be making their abstracts simpler and more straightforward. Perhaps, in doing so, they are cutting extra words – like "novel" and "promising".

What can be done to reduce the "motherhood penalty"?

The "motherhood penalty" – the sharp decline in earnings that women suffer after giving birth – is one of the principal causes of the gender pay gap. It often locks women into lower incomes for the rest of their careers. Governments around the world have sought ways to reduce the opportunity cost of having children, and cause it to be shared more evenly between men and women. A working paper published in May 2019 examines the impact of the introduction of paid maternity leave in Switzerland in 2004. It is a rare comprehensive study of the impact of such policies. It finds that the policy did appear to shrink the motherhood penalty – but by a disappointingly small amount.

In a referendum in September 2004, Swiss voters approved a new law that requires the government to pay mothers 80% of their previous salary for 14 weeks after giving birth, up to a cap of SFR196 ($196) per day. The benefit is funded by a tax on payrolls of 0.45%, split equally between employers and workers. It also protects women against losing their jobs for 16 weeks after their babies are born. Eligibility requirements are strict. To qualify, women must have worked for at least five months of their pregnancy, and still hold a paid job on the day they give birth. Nonetheless, the law's passage made Switzerland the last country in western Europe to guarantee paid maternity leave, and left the United States as the world's only rich economy without such a policy.

The policy has had modest success. The working paper compares mothers' average wages before and after the introduction of paid maternity leave. Surprisingly, the study found that maternity leave actually reduced first-time mothers' average earnings by 4% one year before giving birth. However, it also led to a faster recovery in salaries, such that mothers' wages four years after giving birth were 2% higher than they had been before the policy was enacted.

The authors propose a benign explanation for the apparent negative pre-natal impact on earnings: the introduction of maternity leave may have prompted some women who were not working to join the labour force in low-paid jobs before pregnancy, so reducing average earnings. Nonetheless, the overall post-natal impact of the law, although positive, seems surprisingly small. Previous research from Nordic countries suggests that better paternity leave and a change in social norms regarding the division of child-rearing and housework can help narrow the gap, for instance by allowing women to return to work sooner and thus suffer a shorter interruption to their careers. Fathers may need to work harder at home, it seems, so that mothers can draw level at work.

Does greater access to abortion reduce crime rates?

Anti-abortion policies are on the rise in America. Influenced mainly by objections from religious conservatives, legislators in states such as Georgia, Ohio and Alabama have passed new laws limiting the practice. In some instances, the new regulations go so far as to ban abortions even in cases of rape or incest – a measure supported by just 11% of voters, according to Morning Consult, a pollster. Restricting access to abortions means that more parents who don't want to raise children will be forced to do so. Research suggests this could reverse decades of progress made on curbing crime in America.

In a paper published in 2001, the economists John Donahue and Steven Levitt credited the legalisation of abortion across America with much of the subsequent reduction in crime in the country. They argued that violent crime in states where abortion had been banned before 1973 was 15–25% rarer in 1997 than it would have been had abortion remained illegal. Their study was politically explosive and widely criticised. Many sceptical scholars sought to poke holes in its methods, including one group who discovered an "inadvertent but serious computer programming error" underlying its findings.

Nearly two decades later, Mr Donahue and Mr Levitt returned to the subject with new evidence that bolsters their original claim. In a working paper circulated in 2019 by the National Bureau of Economic Research, they attribute a whopping 45 percentage points of the total 50% decline in crime since 1990 to legal abortion. Their primary evidence is that crime fell much faster in states where more abortions were performed than in those where the procedure was rarer. In the early 1990s violent crime was about 50% more common in states with relatively high abortion levels than in those where abortion was infrequent. By 2014, crime rates in the two groups of states had converged.

The authors argue that this statistical association reflects an

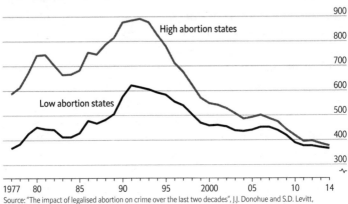

Roe and behold
Violent crimes per 100,000 people

Source: "The impact of legalised abortion on crime over the last two decades", J.J. Donohue and S.D. Levitt, National Bureau of Economic Research, working paper, 2019

underlying causal relationship. Armed with a cache of annual state-level data on abortions, crime rates and other factors – including economic conditions, welfare payments, access to firearms and alcohol consumption – they seek to isolate the impact of abortion on violent crime, after controlling for other variables that also affect crime rates. With all other factors held constant, they find that an increase in the abortion rate of 100 per 100,000 births leads to a 10–20% reduction in crime. Past studies have also shown that children born to women who wanted an abortion but did not receive one were much more likely to become criminals and had poorer life prospects than those who were born to parents ready and willing to raise them.

Why China has so many female billionaires

Dong Mingzhu is the most visible face of female enterprise in China. The 64-year-old boss of Gree, the world's biggest maker of air-conditioners, is everywhere: in television ads, on billboards and, on one occasion in 2018, in two places at once – at Gree's headquarters in Zhuhai, while also jaywalking in the city of Ningbo (police cameras were mistakenly triggered by an image of her face in an advertisement plastered on a passing bus). Ms Dong joined Gree as a door-to-door saleswoman in 1990. In 2012 she became its chairwoman. Her life was the subject of a TV drama, and she has written two popular memoirs. Her steely, unglamorous image (a confessed penchant for skirts notwithstanding) inspires young women. Matters of gender bore her. Asked about her rise in a country run by men, she responds: "Men or women, few are up to the challenge."

That may be so. But Ms Dong represents a generation of Chinese women who have climbed higher than their sisters in South Korea or Japan. Fully 51 of the 89 self-made female billionaires on the 2019 Hurun Rich List, a Who's Who of the ultra-wealthy, were Chinese – well above China's 20% share of the world's women. Relative to population (one for every 13.4m Chinese females), that was not far off America's tally of 18 (one for every 9.1m). China's dozens of female billionaires include Wu Yajun, a property mogul with a $10bn fortune; Cheng Xue of Foshan Haitian Flavouring & Food Company, known as "the soy-sauce queen"; and Li Haiyan and Shu Ping, co-founders of Haidilao, a chain of hotpot restaurants. Ms Dong may be more famous, but with a net worth of a mere 3bn yuan ($440m), she did not make Hurun's list.

Why have China's women done so well? If socialist egalitarianism – which encouraged, even required, women to work – were the whole story, you would expect many women in the upper echelons of the Communist Party. In fact, just one sits on the 25-member Politburo, and none has ever joined the inner sanctum of the Standing Committee. A likelier explanation is

China's manufacturing boom, which gave women unprecedented opportunities. In 1968 Mao Zedong enjoined female labourers to hold up "half the sky"; by the 1980s their labour-force participation hovered around 80%. Britain's then stood at 60%, and America's lower still. India, with a similar GDP per person to China at the time, barely managed 30%. Many successful Chinese businesswomen rose from the factory floor. In 2015 Zhou Qunfei, an erstwhile migrant worker who went on to found Lens Technology, a maker of screens for Apple, took the title of the world's wealthiest self-made woman. Women make up 56% of Chinese graduates, even though only 87 girls are born for every 100 boys (the world's most unbalanced sex ratio). According to the Global Entrepreneurship Monitor, an index of startup activity, for every ten men starting a business in China, eight women do the same.

All that ought to guarantee a steady supply of talent to follow in Ms Dong's footsteps. But it may be stymied by a general slowdown in the pace of female progress. Between 2010 and 2018 China dropped from 61st (among 134 countries) to 103rd (out of 149) in the World Economic Forum's Gender Gap Report. Normally, economic disparities between the sexes narrow as countries grow richer. China's have widened, as women have moved into lower-paying service jobs or left the workforce. Relative to that of men, female participation has been flat or fallen every year since 2009, to 69%, similar to Japan and below Vietnam, Cambodia and Laos. Female wages, which were 17% below male wages in the early 1990s, are now 36% lower. Women also face discrimination in China's fast-growing and male-dominated tech industry. Hurun's list of 46 self-made billionaires under the age of 40 includes 16 Chinese founders. Only two of them – both wives in couples who launched internet platforms – are women.

Why more Africans are marrying spouses of different ethnicities

In 2018 a dating app was launched targeting African diasporas in America. CultureCrush was described by its founder as an "inclusive ecosystem". The app promised to be the first to allow users looking for love to search for mates by "nationality, ethnicity and tribe". For lonely hearts in Chicago or New York that may well be a useful feature. But in Africa, love, or at least marriage, is increasingly transcending ethnic boundaries. Several studies find that it is becoming more common for Africans to get hitched to partners from other groups.

A paper published in January 2020 by Juliette Crespin-Boucaud of the Paris School of Economics found that the share of marriages that are "interethnic" ranged from 10% of the total in Burkina Faso to 46% in Zambia. The average share in the 15 countries she looked at was 20%. Another study, published as a working paper in 2018 by Sanghamitra Bandyopadhyay of Queen Mary University in London and Elliott Green of the London School of Economics, found a similar figure among a sample of 26 countries: 22%. All the researchers found that younger generations were more likely to ignore ethnic barriers. About 17% of women's first marriages in 1984 were interethnic, rising to 26% in 2014, according to Ms Bandyopadhyay and Mr Green.

Urbanisation is one reason for the change. In cities there are more people from different backgrounds with whom to consort than in villages. It is harder for nosy relatives to interfere. Education matters, too. More schooling means higher incomes and more choice. Yet these are not the only factors, says Ms Crespin-Boucaud. Changing cultural attitudes are important too. These days marrying outside one's group is less likely to be taboo. Why this has happened faster in some countries (such as Uganda) than others (such as Niger) is unclear.

Whatever the reasons, boundary-spanning marriages are good news, and not just for the happy couples. Another paper, published in 2018 by Boniface Dulani of the University of Malawi and three co-authors, suggests that children of mixed marriages are less likely to vote along ethnic lines. Ethnically driven politics has been blamed for many African woes, from conflict to corruption. So if love can blur those boundaries, all the better.

Can attractive Airbnb hosts charge more?

Pretty people have all the luck. Studies show that the good-looking are considered more likeable, more intelligent and more employable than the rest of the population. They also earn more. A paper published in 1994 found that attractive men were paid 5% more than average-looking ones; attractive women made 4% more. In peer-to-peer marketplaces such as Airbnb and Uber, where buyers and sellers interact directly with one another, first impressions are particularly important. And research confirms that such online platforms are, in part, beauty contests.

In a paper published in December 2019 in the *Journal of Economic Psychology*, researchers at Tilburg University and the University of Twente, both in the Netherlands, asked individuals recruited from Amazon's Mechanical Turk, a crowd-working platform, to rate more than 1,000 flats in New York City listed on Airbnb. Each listing on the accommodation-rental service was evaluated according to the attractiveness and perceived trustworthiness of the host's profile picture, on an 11-point scale ranging from "not at all" to "extremely". These ratings were compared to the price of a stay.

The authors found that, after controlling for factors such as location and property size, a one-point increase in a host's attractiveness rating was associated with a 2.8% increase in rental prices. But this was not a "beauty premium", whereby hotter hosts command higher-than-average prices. Instead, unattractive hosts suffered an "ugliness penalty", earning 6.8% less for their listings. People with trustworthy-looking faces also turned out to charge slightly less than their shiftier-looking peers, perhaps confirming their presumed honesty.

Airbnb bias goes beyond attractiveness, however. The authors also ran the 1,000-odd profile photos through an algorithm that classified hosts by race, age and "smile intensity". They found that Airbnb renters are willing to pay 3.6% more to stay with a grinning host than a sullen one. Black hosts, meanwhile, earn 10.1% less for their apartments than white hosts. A study published in 2014 found

In the eyes of the bed-holder

New York City, effect of Airbnb host and apartment characteristics on rental price, %

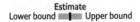

Estimate
Lower bound ▬▮▬ Upper bound

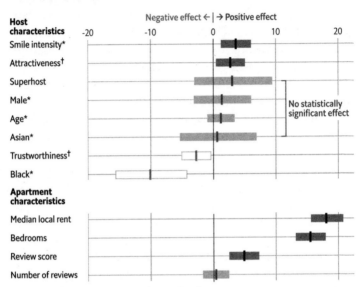

Source: "The effects of facial attractiveness and trustworthiness in online peer-to-peer markets", B. Jaeger *et al.*, *Journal of Economic Psychology*, 2019

*Assessed by algorithm
†Assessed by Mechanical Turk recruits

a similar penalty for black hosts in New York, calling it a form of digital discrimination. Brian Chesky, Airbnb's boss, has said such prejudice is "the greatest challenge we face as a company". The firm has set up a special team of engineers and researchers to tackle racial bias, and asked its users to sign an anti-discrimination agreement. But if these findings are anything to go by, such discrimination takes many forms.

Why art by women sells at a discount

A rose painted by another name would cost more. In a paper published in 2019, a group led by Renée Adams of Oxford University showed that art made by women sold for lower prices at auction than art made by men, and suggested that this discount had nothing to do with talent or thematic choices. It was solely because the artists were female. The authors used a sample of 1.9m transactions in art auctions across 49 countries in the period from 1970 to 2016. They found that art made by women sold at an average discount of 42% compared with works by men. However, auction prices can be distorted by a few famous artists whose output is perceived as extremely valuable. Once transactions above $1m were excluded, the discount fell to 19%. But that gap still demands explanation.

One possibility is that women choose different subjects. This is partly true; for example, a higher proportion of women than men paint roses, whereas a smaller share create landscapes. But it turns out that themes that are more associated with female artists sell at a premium, not a discount. Indeed, the researchers could not explain the female discount in terms of other factors such as the size, style or medium of the works, or the age of the artist. Another possibility could be that women are just less talented than men. To test that proposition, the authors conducted a couple of experiments. In one, they showed 1,000 people a selection of ten lesser-known paintings and asked them to guess the gender of the artists. The respondents were right only 50.5% of the time, no better than tossing a coin. In short, the general public cannot tell the difference between male and female art.

In another test, the researchers used a computer program to generate paintings and randomly assign the results to artists with male or female names. They then asked participants to rate the paintings and ascribe a value. The experiment found that affluent individuals (those most likely to bid at auctions) attributed a lower value to works which the program assigned to a woman. Clearly, this gap was unrelated to the artistic merit of the pictures. It could be that these well-heeled observers were aware of the market discount for female artists, and applied it accordingly. But that does not solve the puzzle of why the gulf opened up in the first place. Two more findings imply that the difference relates to culture rather than talent. First, the academics considered the relationship between the female discount and the level of gender inequality in the countries where the auctions took place, based on indices of educational attainment and political empowerment. The average discount applied to the work of a given female artist was lowest in countries where women were more equal. (There were some exceptions to the rule, such as Brazil, where women's art was highly rated.)

The good news is that the female discount has fallen over time. For transactions under $1m, the study calculated, the discount fell from 33% in the 1970s to 8% after 2010. That once again confirms that ability never had anything to do with the disparity. But the reduction in the discount has another implication. As it has shrunk, so the returns on women's art have grown; since the 1970s they have been higher than for their male peers. Collectors should put aside their prejudices. As the art world's ingrained chauvinism abates, the female of the species has become a better investment than the male.

Culinary oddities: food and drink

What's driving the surge in interest in veganism?

For years Britons intent on a virtuous start to the year have pledged to observe an alcohol-free "Dry January". These days, however, a trendier resolution is to swear off meat. In January 2020, according to Google Trends, there were for the first time about as many British searches for "Veganuary" – in which participants adopt a vegan diet for a month – as for "Dry January". Veganuary UK, the charity behind the annual campaign, says 350,000 signed up for it in 2020, compared with 250,000 in 2019. Just how many have stuck to their commitment is anyone's guess. But enthusiasm for veganism is not limited to Britain.

If Google searches are any guide, interest in the plant-based diet has surged in recent years across much of the rich world. Since 2015, searches for "veganism" have doubled in America and tripled in Australia, France and Spain. In Sweden, home to the climate activist Greta Thunberg, searches have more than quadrupled. Eating habits are changing, too. Ipsos MORI, a pollster, reckons that the number of vegans in Britain quadrupled between 2014 and 2018, from 150,000 to 600,000, a little over 1% of the adult population. In America roughly 2% of adults consider themselves vegans, according to YouGov, another pollster. Another 5% identify as vegetarians and 3% as pescatarians.

But the notion of part-time veganism – implicit in a pledge of a meat-free month, or "vegan before six" (a form of part-time veganism that does not extend to dinnertime) – is controversial. For staunch vegans who abstain from animal products for ethical reasons, killing animals is wrong at all times of the day and on every day of the year. Surveys suggest, however, that newcomers to veganism are less interested in animal welfare, and are more concerned about perceived health benefits or environmental impact.

This suggests that part-time veganism will grow in popularity. According to YouGov, about 59% of Americans who were eating

A chance of meatballs

Google search interest in "veganism" by country, 100=max

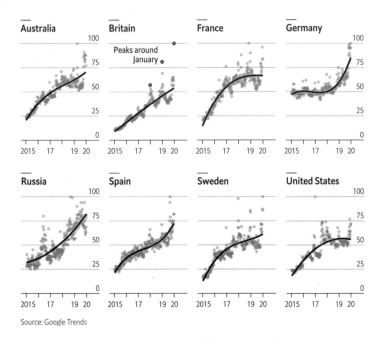

Source: Google Trends

less meat than they did a year ago were doing so mainly for health reasons; another 10% cited climate change as their primary motivation. Just 9% were cutting back out of concern for animal welfare. Among those aged 18 to 29, concern about the climate was much higher, at 24%. Among this younger group, only 5% cited animal welfare as the reason for eating less meat – even less than the 6% of respondents who said they had cut back "because it is trendy".

How Uber facilitates heavy drinking

Uber has hit a few potholes on its journey to becoming the world's leading ride-hailing company. In recent years it has been beset by sexual-harassment scandals, lawsuits over drivers' contracts and battles with regulators. Its share price fell in the months after it went public in May 2019. After all these bumps, it is easy to forget just how much urbanites around the world have come to rely on Uber, which now serves more than 700 cities.

Among other things, Uber has made it far easier for party-goers to get home safely. A study published in 2017 found that after Uber's arrival in Portland, Oregon, alcohol-related car crashes declined by 62%. But at the same time, the spread of ride-hailing apps may have tempted people to drink to excess, knowing that they won't be at the wheel. A study published in November 2019 by three economists – Jacob Burgdorf and Conor Lennon of the University of Louisville, and Keith Teltser of Georgia State University – found that the widespread availability of ride-sharing apps had indeed made it easier for the late-night crowd to binge.

By matching data on Uber's availability with health surveys from America's Centres for Disease Control and Prevention, the authors found that on average alcohol consumption rose by 3%, binge drinking (in which a person downs four or five drinks in two hours) increased by 8%, and heavy drinking (defined as three or more instances of binge drinking in a month) surged by 9% within a couple of years of the ride-hailing company coming to town. Increases were even higher in cities without public transport, where the presence of Uber led average drinking to rise by 5% and instances of binge drinking to go up by around 20%. (Heavy drinking still rose by 9%.) Remarkably, excessive drinking had actually been in decline before Uber's appearance, giving further evidence that the firm's arrival affected behaviour.

If people are likelier to drink a lot, but less likely to drive drunk, it is hard to say what the overall public-health impact of ride-hailing firms has been. That said, there is one group of individuals who have undoubtedly benefited from the presence of Uber, Lyft and others: bartenders. Messrs Burgdorf, Lennon and Teltser find that employment at bars and restaurants increases by an average of 2% whenever Uber enters the market.

Why responsible drinking would bankrupt the drinks industry

Of all the substances people intoxicate themselves with, alcohol is the least restricted and causes the most harm. Many illegal drugs are more dangerous to those who use them, but are relatively hard to obtain, which limits their impact. By contrast, alcohol is omnipresent, so far more people suffer from its adverse effects. In 2010 a group of drug experts scored the total harm in Britain caused by 20 common intoxicants and concluded that alcohol inflicted the greatest cost, mostly because of the damage it does to non-consumers, such as the victims of drunk drivers (see "What is the most dangerous drug?", page 146).

No Western country has banned alcohol since America repealed Prohibition in 1933. It is popular and easy to produce. As America's experience showed, making it illegal enriches criminals and starts turf wars. In recent years governments have begun legalising other drugs. And to limit the harm caused by alcohol, they have tried to dissuade people from drinking using taxes, awareness campaigns and limits on where, when and to whom booze can be sold.

The alcohol industry has pitched itself as part of the solution. In Britain more than 100 producers and retailers have signed a "responsibility deal" and promised to "help people to drink within guidelines", mostly by buying ads promoting moderation. But if these campaigns were effective, they would ruin their sponsors' finances. According to researchers from the University of Sheffield and the Institute of Alcohol Studies, a think-tank, some two-fifths of alcohol consumed in Britain is in excess of the recommended weekly maximum of 14 units (about one glass of wine per day). Industry executives say they want the public to "drink less, but drink better", meaning fewer, fancier tipples. But people would need to pay 22–98% more per drink to make up for the revenue loss that such a steep drop in consumption would cause.

Health officials have taken note of such arithmetic. Some now wonder if Big Booze is sincere in its efforts to discourage boozing.

In 2018 America's National Institutes of Health stopped a $100m study of moderate drinking, which was partly funded by alcohol firms, because its design was biased in their products' favour. And in 2019 the World Health Organisation and England's public-health authority banned their staff from working with the industry. Producers are ready to fend off regulators. In 1999 alcohol firms invested half as much on lobbying in America as tobacco firms did. Now they spend 31% more.

Which countries' cuisines are the most popular abroad?

"The destiny of nations", wrote Jean Anthelme Brillat-Savarin, an 18th-century French gastronome, "depends on how they nourish themselves." Today a nation's stature depends on how well it nourishes the rest of the world, too. For proof of this, consider the rise of culinary diplomacy. In 2012 America's State Department launched a "chef corps" tasked with promoting American cuisine abroad. Thailand's government sends chefs overseas to peddle pad thai and massaman curry through its Global Thai programme. South Korea pursues its own brand of "kimchi diplomacy".

But which country's cuisine is at the top of the global food chain? A paper published in 2019 in the *Journal of Cultural Economics* provides an answer. Using restaurant listings from TripAdvisor, a travel-review website, and sales figures from Euromonitor, a market-research firm, Joel Waldfogel of the University of Minnesota estimates the extent of world "trade" in cuisines for 52 countries. Whereas traditional trade is measured based on the value of goods and services that flow across a country's borders, the author's estimates of culinary exchange are based on the value of food found on restaurant tables. Domestic consumption of foreign cuisine is treated as an "import", whereas foreign consumption of domestic cuisine is treated as an "export". The balance determines which countries have the greatest influence on the world's palate.

The results make grim reading for America's McDonald's-munching, tariff-touting president. The United States is the world's biggest net importer of cuisine, gobbling down $55bn more in foreign dishes than the rest of the world eats in American fare (when fast food is excluded, this figure balloons to $134bn). China comes next, with a $52bn dietary deficit; Brazil and Britain have shortfalls worth around $34bn and $30bn respectively. Italy, meanwhile, ranks as the world's biggest exporter of edibles. The world's enormous appetite for pasta and pizza, coupled with Italians' relative indifference to other cuisines, gives the country

Unbalanced diets
Cuisine "net exports", 2017, $bn

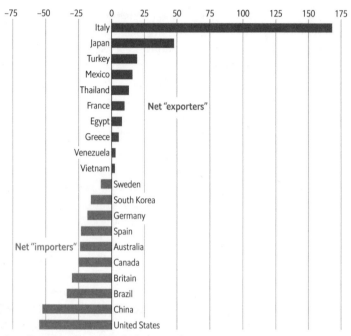

Source: "Dining out as cultural trade", J. Waldfogel, *Journal of Cultural Economics*, 2019

a $168bn surplus. Japan, Turkey and Mexico also boast robust surpluses, for similar reasons.

Mr Waldfogel does not account for culinary hybrids such as the cronut – a cross between a croissant and a doughnut – or Tex-Mex cuisine. Nor does he consider authenticity; few Neapolitans would consider Domino's Pizza a real taste of home. Even so, it is clear that some cuisines have a bigger worldwide appeal than others. Foodies scoffing spring rolls in San Francisco or cheeseburgers in Chongqing should give thanks to globalisation. A policy of culinary mercantilism would make dining out very dull indeed.

Proof that cannabis really does give you the munchies

It is common knowledge that smoking marijuana causes cravings for high-calorie snacks. The condition, known as the munchies, is a staple of popular culture. (Snoop Dogg, a rapper and notorious stoner, has even penned a cookbook.) Yet empirical evidence of the phenomenon and its effects is scarce. Does getting high cause smokers to consume more junk food? And if so, by how much? To answer this question, Michele Baggio of the University of Connecticut and Alberto Chong of Georgia State University examined state laws in America. Since the mid-1990s, more than 30 states have authorised marijuana for medical purposes and 11 have legalised it for recreational use. Because these laws were enacted at different times and in different places, they created a natural experiment for researchers to study the effects of marijuana – including its effect on food consumption.

With this in mind, Mr Baggio and Mr Chong collected monthly sales data from supermarkets, drug stores and other retailers in more than 2,000 counties across 48 states, covering the period from 2006 to 2016. By comparing sales figures from neighbouring counties located along state borders – some where marijuana was legal and some where it was not – the authors were able to estimate the effect of marijuana legalisation on junk-food sales. They found that after recreational marijuana was legalised in Colorado, Oregon and Washington, the only states for which 18 months of sales data were available, sales of ice-cream rose by 3.1%, sales of cookies increased by 4.1% and sales of crisps jumped by 5.3% in the years after the laws were passed.

Marijuana may affect shopping habits in other ways, too. In another paper, Mr Baggio and Mr Chong, along with Sungoh Kwon of the University of Connecticut, found that legalising medical marijuana reduced alcohol sales by more than 12%. This "substitution effect" was larger than previously thought and lasted for up to two years after legalisation. One explanation for this

Hey hey we're the munchies

United States, effect of recreational marijuana laws on junk-food sales, %

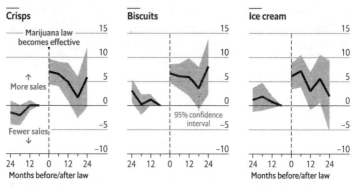

Source: "Recreational marijuana laws and junk food consumption: evidence using border analysis and retail sales data", M. Baggio and A. Chong, International Centre for Public Policy, working paper, 2019

effect may be that some people use alcohol to treat pain. When medical marijuana becomes available, they swap one pain-reliever for another. A sensible approach, perhaps, given the relative harm posed by excessive alcohol use. Those watching their weight, however, may want to avoid the snack aisle.

How beer snobs drink beers they claim to dislike

Carlsberg, a Danish brewery, used to boast that its lager was "probably the best beer in the world". No longer. In March 2019 it began selling a new pilsner – a pale, Czech-style lager – after admitting that drinkers had soured on its original recipe. Data from Untappd, a beer-rating site with 7m (mostly American) users, confirm that pontificating pint-swillers are turning their noses up at mass-market lager. Among the 5,000 beers its users reported drinking most often, lagers (made with "bottom-fermenting" yeast, which yields a light-bodied, mild brew) are rated 3.29 out of 5 on average. The rest get an average of 3.69. Moreover, the lagers that Untappd users like the most do not taste like lager. When grouped by the words in Untappd descriptions (many copied from labels), the best-rated terms are ones mostly used for ale, such as "tropical" and "dark". Yet despite such poor reviews, the specific beers that Untappd users say they drink most often turn out to be lagers. What is going on?

A big part of the explanation is fragmentation. Though reported consumption tends to be higher for individual lagers than for ales, there are far more ales than lagers, so ale consumption is spread out over a larger number of beers, making them appear individually less popular than lagers – even though ales account for 73% of drinking of the 5,000 leading beers recorded on Untappd. Among the American population as a whole, mass-market lager outsells craft beer by a factor of six to one, according to IWSR, a research firm. Most drinkers, in other words, are not beer snobs, and even ale devotees might secretly enjoy a frosty lager on a hot day. And most importantly, lagers dominate supply chains. Craft ales may abound at organic grocers and hipster bars, but Carlsberg (rated 2.96) and Budweiser (2.54) are everywhere.

Low costs originally gave lager its distribution advantage. Its cold-fermentation process translates well to large batches, and using fewer hops saves money. In the 19th century these economies of scale let big firms flood America with watery lager. Prohibition reinforced this pattern: most craft breweries closed down for good, whereas large producers resumed brewing afterwards. In recent years, however, the market as a whole has inched closer to Untappd users' preferences. Between 2010 and 2018 American consumption of mass-market lager fell by 12.5%, while that of craft beer doubled – even though craft costs 67% more than lager on average. Unfortunately for the beer industry, it sells so much lager that this switch has hurt it. Overall revenues in America are down by 9% in real terms since 2010. Giants like Carlsberg face an extra obstacle. Even if they launch or buy a rich, craft-style ale, it may be shunned by beer snobs because it was made by a behemoth.

Why Americans pay more for lunch than Britons do

In the summer of 2019 Pret A Manger, purveyor of sandwiches to desk-workers in the white-collar cities of the West, added lobster rolls to its menu. In Britain they cost £5.99 ($7.31); in America $9.99. In both countries they were filled with lobster from Maine, along with cucumber, mayonnaise and more. Rent and labour cost about the same in London as in downtown New York or Boston. Neither sticker price includes sales tax. Yet a Pret lobster roll in America is a third pricier than in Britain, even though the lobster comes from nearer by.

This Pret price gap is not limited to lobster rolls. According to data gathered by *The Economist* on the dozen Pret sandwiches that are most similar in the two countries, the American ones cost on average 74% more. An egg sandwich in New York costs $4.99 to London's £1.79, more than double. A tuna baguette costs two-thirds more. The price mismatch is intriguing – the more so for *The Economist*, which publishes the Big Mac index, a cross-country comparison of burger prices.

Menu pricing starts with a simple rule, says John Buchanan of the consulting arm of Lettuce Entertain You Enterprises, a restaurant group: take the cost of ingredients and multiply by three. Then ask yourself how much customers would expect to pay for a dish of this type, and how much they would expect to pay for it from you. A Pret lobster roll and one from a fancy seafood restaurant are quite different propositions. Lastly, check what the competition charges. "Only a small part of this decision is what I would call scientific," says Mr Buchanan. "A lot has to do with a subjective judgment of what the market will bear."

The lunch market is local. New Yorkers do not care about prices in London. And they – alongside Bostonians and Washingtonians – are used to their local high prices, for reasons that include bigger portions (though not at Pret) and tipping habits. Londoners, meanwhile, are keener on sandwich lunches, which means stiffer competition in that part of the market. Often lunch prices vary by neighbourhood. JD Wetherspoon, a British pub chain, prides itself on low prices, but allows them to differ by branch. In 2017 the *Financial Times* found that the most expensive Wetherspoon branches charged over 40% more than the cheapest ones. Prices also vary by time: many restaurants charge more for dinner than for lunch. Perceptions of value for money are relative not absolute. For Pret's lobster rolls, it's a case of claws and effect.

Why America still has "dry" counties

June 5th is National Moonshine Day, when American tipplers lift a mason jar to the illegal liquor that got them through Prohibition. For most drinkers, that world of bootleggers and secret stills is just a part of history. But roughly 18m Americans still live in "dry" counties or municipalities, where the sale of alcohol is banned by law. How have these holdouts survived into modern times, and what are the consequences for people who live there?

Parts of the United States were dry even before the start of Prohibition. Maine implemented its own anti-booze rules as early as the 1840s. In 1919, the 18th amendment spread these restrictions nationwide. Although many Americans lamented the ban – and dodged it by getting legal whisky prescribed by doctors – others rejoiced. Some Protestants saw boozing as sinful, while others fretted about the social dangers of letting immigrants and the poor get drunk. These attitudes persisted even after 1933, when President Franklin D. Roosevelt switched on the taps again. Several states maintained their own prohibitions. Mississippi bars only reopened their doors in the 1960s. As late as 2006, South Carolinians visiting a local bar could only buy shots from tiny bottles better suited to an airliner's drinks trolley.

Statewide bans on alcohol have now disappeared. But around 10% of the country, by area, keeps up local restrictions, especially in the South. Five counties in Texas and 34 in Arkansas are still dry. Rules in parts of Alaska are so strict that the mere possession of alcohol is illegal. Even so-called "moist" counties only permit drinking in certain areas, or limit drinking in other ways (by restricting alcohol sales to large restaurants, for example). Though campaigners try to loosen rules – in 2016 Alabamians voted to abolish their last teetotal county – change can be slow. This is partly social. Americans might be more liberal than they were in 1919, but cautious attitudes remain. A culture of abstinence has had a lasting residual impact. Legal hurdles hardly help. Thirsty citizens in Arkansas can only get Prohibition repeal on a ballot if

38% of voters in any given jurisdiction sign a petition, whereas other issues qualify for a referendum with just 15%. Some drinkers even sabotage repeal efforts themselves. Bootleggers in a dry corner of Alaska, worried their business would collapse, plied voters with free drink to persuade them to vote against going legally wet.

These desperate tactics are unsurprising: Prohibition still offers space for unscrupulous vendors to get rich. At the Pine Ridge Indian Reservation, near South Dakota's border with Nebraska, bootleggers sell beers for $3 and vodka (mixed with hand sanitiser) for $10. Prohibition can be dangerous in other ways, too. Because people in dry areas need to travel for a fix, drunk-driving accidents are far more common. For homebodies, drug-abuse rates can increase. Researchers at the University of Louisville found that dry counties in Kentucky were nearly twice as likely to be caught hosting illegal meth labs as their wet neighbours. No wonder punters from Kansas to Maryland have voted to relax Prohibition in recent years. If for no other reason, letting in the booze makes financial sense. One study from 2014 found that turning three dry Arkansas counties wet could bring in over $30m a year to the local economy – good cause for cracking open a bottle or three.

Why Eid is a movable feast for Muslims

The month of Ramadan can be arduous for fasting Muslims, and Eid al-Fitr, the celebration of the month's culmination, is eagerly anticipated. To mark a return to prandial normality, Muslims feast and revel with family. But they are not united in celebration. Muslims celebrate on different days, with divisions arising not only between countries, but within communities and even families. There are even anecdotal stories of calendrical fistfights breaking out in mosques. It seems bizarre that the simple determination of a religious festival is marred by such intense controversy. Why is there such disagreement over the date of Eid?

The issue is linked to Islam's lack of a central religious authority. In Muslim countries, the date of Eid is decided by a government, court or related body; in non-Muslim countries the decision is taken by individual mosques. Islam uses the lunar calendar, where the start of each month coincides with the birth of a new moon. Determining this occurrence is not straightforward. Many scholars believe the month does not begin when the new moon is born, but when its crescent can be seen by the naked eye. On the night when the moon is expected to be visible, meteorological committees and ordinary people alike will turn questing looks to the skies. But this reliance on concrete sightings means that something as simple as a cloudy night can delay Eid by a day. Other scholars, motivated by a less literal reading of the Koran, argue that Muslims ought to make use of modern science. The Fiqh Council of North America and the European Council for Fatwa and Research, two associations of Muslim clerics, say astronomical calculation is an acceptable methodology, which means that dates are known years in advance. They have led attempts to create a universal Islamic calendar, but to little avail.

Even among those who require sightings of the moon there is further disagreement. Some demand local sightings, but others feel an allegiance to Saudi Arabia, both spiritually and, thanks to the kingdom's massive funding programme for mosques and religious schools, financially. Many mosques will therefore align their calendars with those of Mecca. But racial separation within the Islamic community means mosques with congregations made up largely of immigrants from the Indian subcontinent will often follow the decisions of Pakistani or Indian authorities instead. This ensures that multinational families are synchronised, but by fragmenting Muslim communities in towns with multiple mosques, it can reinforce national tribalism.

The moon-sighting debate reflects wider divides in Islam. Different ideologies jostle for control, with Western modernists pushing for change against Saudi Arabia's staunch traditionalism. Younger Muslims may be taking matters into their own hands: Google searches for "moon sighting" spike before each Eid. But as long as Islam remains decentralised and the Koran ambiguous, it is unlikely that Muslims will ever agree.

Why Italians are up in arms about Nutella

In the distance, Orvieto's cathedral sits majestically on the massive outcrop over which the city spreads. Nearby, at the edge of the Alfina plateau, stands a castle encircled by fields – part of the landscape, between Orvieto and Lake Bolsena, in which Alice Rohrwacher, an Italian director, set her prize-winning film *The Wonders*. After a long absence, Ms Rohrwacher returned to find it transformed. "Fields, hedges and trees [had vanished] to make way for hazel plantations as far as the eye could see," she wrote to the regional governors of Umbria and neighbouring Lazio.

Around the castle, 200 hectares are earmarked for intensive hazelnut cultivation, says Vittorio Fagioli, a local environmentalist. This is largely to satisfy the world's appetite for Nutella, the sugary nut-and-chocolate gloop that has helped transform the producer, Ferrero, into a multinational with turnover of more than €10bn ($11bn) a year. Under a deal signed with a local farming consortium, 700 hectares are to be given over by 2023 to the growing of hazelnuts. It is part of a plan to boost the area in Italy devoted to hazelnuts from 70,000 to 90,000 hectares, extending it for the first time to Umbria and other regions.

On the Alfina plateau, however, the firm's strategy has met vigorous opposition. According to Mr Fagioli, each tree will need 30 litres of water a day, pesticides to deter insects and fertilisers to boost yields. Campaigners fear that all those chemicals will drain into Lake Bolsena, since it receives most of its water from the plateau. They look apprehensively at Lake Vico in Lazio, ringed for decades by hazel plantations, where in 2009 a build-up of chemicals produced carcinogenic algae that required the installation of a costly water-treatment plant. Ferrero disagrees, saying that hazelnut cultivation around Lake Bolsena is "marginal" and that crops such as olives, grapes and apples need even more chemicals. In other words: nuts to you. Nutella is easily spread. Will the same be true of environmental opposition to hazelnut cultivation?

How Burgundy wine investors beat the stockmarket

Wine collectors like to proclaim that "all roads lead to Burgundy". They often wince at the plonk they drank when starting their hobby. In America and Australia, a common entry point is local "fruit bombs": heavy, alcoholic wines that taste of plum or blackberry, bear the vanilla or mocha imprint of oak barrels and should be drunk within a few years of bottling. As oenophiles gain experience, they begin to see the merits of lower-octane French options: Cabernet Sauvignon from Bordeaux rather than Napa; Rhône Syrah instead of Barossa Shiraz. But once you start to value complexity and finesse over power, your vinous destination is pre-ordained.

Encyclopaedic wine knowledge is most precious in Burgundy. The French region is split into hundreds of named vineyards. In turn, myriad producers own specific rows within each vineyard, from which they all make unique wines. This yields thousands of distinct pairings, each consisting of a few thousand bottles at most. Moreover, red Burgundy is made from Pinot Noir, a grape with a maddening ageing pattern. After a few years of storage, it tends to "shut down" and lose flavour. The best wines blossom after a few decades, but many never "wake up" from their slumber.

In the past, Burgundy's complexity and small output relegated it to a market niche. A decade ago, Bordeaux – which makes fewer distinct wines in larger batches – became popular in Asia, and prices soared. But the bubble burst in 2012, when China's government began to frown on lavish gifts. As tastes moved on from commoditised Bordeaux, mastery of Burgundy became seen as the test of connoisseurship, both in Asia and the West. But the region's vast array of wines – including trophies as scarce as 300 bottles a year – makes reliable pricing data hard to find. Among the hundreds of fine red Burgundies, Liv-ex, a marketplace for the wine trade, includes just 11 in its regional index.

To create a sturdier measure, WineBid, the biggest online wine auctioneer, kindly gave *The Economist* a full sales record for every

Red Burgundy is the only wine category whose returns have beaten the stockmarket since 2003

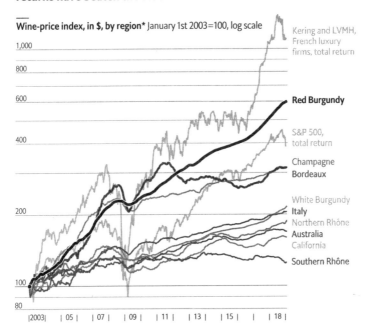

Wine-price index, in $, by region* January 1st 2003=100, log scale

Kering and LVMH, French luxury firms, total return

Red Burgundy

S&P 500, total return

Champagne
Bordeaux

White Burgundy
Italy
Northern Rhône
Australia
California

Southern Rhône

|2003| | 05 | | 07 | | 09 | | 11 | | 13 | | 15 | | | 18 |

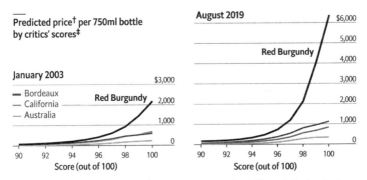

Predicted price† per 750ml bottle by critics' scores‡

August 2019

Red Burgundy

January 2003

— Bordeaux
— California
— Australia

Red Burgundy

Score (out of 100)

Score (out of 100)

*Red only, except Burgundy and Champagne †Calculated using a statistical model ‡Burgundy: Burghound and Stephen Tanzer (all scores raised by one point); Bordeaux and California: *Wine Advocate* (WA), *Wine Spectator* (WS) and Tanzer; Australia: WA and WS Sources: WineBid; *The Economist*

wine sold at least ten times on its site since 2003. The data contain 1.6m lots, covering 33,000 wines. We built portfolios of 50–500 of the most expensive unique labels (one vintage of one wine) from each region. We then estimated the returns for each portfolio, before storage and transaction costs. Collectors who have drunk most of their Pinot already may need another glass after seeing the results. Between 2003 and 2018, red Burgundy returned 497%, versus 279% for the S&P 500. Bordeaux and Champagne rose by 214% over that period; everywhere else did worse. That said, Kering and LVMH – luxury conglomerates whose owners have bought Burgundy vineyards – did even better, returning 958% between 2003 and 2018. The best way to make money from Burgundy would appear to be making wine, not buying it.

Medically speaking: health, death and disease

Why Americans' lives are getting shorter

Two data points, it is often said, do not make a trend. Researchers studying America's dismal life expectancy now have three. After climbing gradually over the past half century, life expectancy in America reached a plateau in 2010 and then fell for three consecutive years from 2015 to 2017, the latest for which data are available. An American baby born today can expect to live 78.6 years, on average, down from 78.9 in 2014. A paper by researchers at Virginia Commonwealth University, published in November 2019 in the *Journal of the American Medical Association*, attempts to explain why.

The prevailing wisdom is that rising mortality in America can be blamed in large part on a handful of causes, including drug overdoses, alcohol-related illnesses and suicides. Such "deaths of despair", the argument goes, are concentrated mainly among whites living in economically depressed regions. The authors of the paper do indeed estimate that mortality from drug overdoses among adults aged 25 to 64 increased by 386.5% between 1999 and 2017. Deaths from alcoholic liver disease jumped by 40.6% during this period, while suicides rose by 38.3%. But the authors note that mortality has increased across 35 causes of death, suggesting that the problem is systemic. Moreover, all racial and ethnic groups have been affected.

Some groups have been affected more than others, however. Young people have been hit especially hard. Between 2010 and 2017, the mortality rate increased by 6% among all working-age adults (from 328.5 to 348.2 deaths per 100,000 population). Among those aged 25 to 34, it jumped by 29% (from 102.9 to 132.8). Adults with less education have also experienced a big rise in mortality. Geography provides another clue. Of the 33,000 "excess deaths" that occurred in America between 2010 and 2017 – defined as the deaths attributed to the change in the mortality rate each year – a third happened in Ohio, Pennsylvania, Indiana and Kentucky, even though those four states are home to just a tenth of the national population.

Dropping off

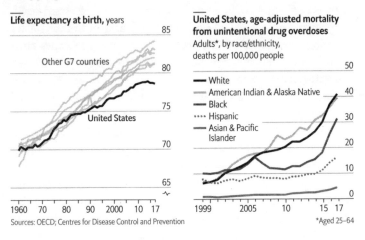

Life expectancy at birth, years

Other G7 countries

United States

85
80
75
70
65

1960 70 80 90 2000 10 17

United States, age-adjusted mortality from unintentional drug overdoses
Adults*, by race/ethnicity, deaths per 100,000 people

— White
— American Indian & Alaska Native
— Black
···· Hispanic
— Asian & Pacific Islander

50
40
30
20
10
0

1999 2005 10 15 17

Sources: OECD; Centres for Disease Control and Prevention   *Aged 25–64

Such regional disparities suggest that not all Americans are doomed to live shorter lives. Life expectancies in the country's most populous states (California, Texas and New York) have changed little since 2010. In coastal areas, they have improved at roughly the same rate as in Canada. Still, many of the underlying causes of higher mortality in America, such as economic distress, are likely to persist. The current trend in Americans' life expectancy may continue for many data points to come.

How China plans to tackle its obesity crisis

In 1926 Walter Mallory, a foreign-affairs expert who would go on to head the Council on Foreign Relations, dubbed China the "land of famine". Nearly a century later, the country is grappling with the opposite problem. More than a quarter of Chinese adults, or roughly 350m people, are overweight or obese; among children, the proportion is one in five, up from just one in 20 in 1995.

China's fat is not spread evenly, however. According to a paper in the *Annals of Internal Medicine*, a journal published by the American College of Physicians, one in seven of the country's adults is obese, defined by Chinese standards as having a body mass index (BMI) of 28 or more. But obesity rates are even higher in big cities, particularly in the north. A quarter of Beijing's adults are considered obese; more than a fifth of adults in Tianjin, a nearby port city, similarly have worrying waistlines. Meanwhile in Guangxi, an agricultural province in the south, less than 6% of adults are obese. In Hainan, a tropical island off China's southern coast, the obesity rate is also below 6%.

Urban living is partly to blame. City dwellers have greater access to Western foods, including those rich in fats and sugars, and tend to lead more sedentary lifestyles. Northern Chinese are more likely than those in the south to consume cereals, high-fat foods and alcohol, all of which help pack on the pounds.

China's government is trying to tackle the problem, though it could do more. Most public-health initiatives – such as "Happy Ten Minutes", a programme which encourages youngsters to exercise for ten minutes a day – emphasise the importance of physical activity but say little about diet. This may not be an accident. Some academics have pointed to the influence in Chinese public-health campaigns of research institutes financed by Western multinational food-and-drink firms such as Nestlé and Coca-Cola. Cutting out junk food would mean slimming down their sales. Instead, ever more Chinese are turning to boot camps, liposuction and diet pills. The country is growing fatter. But official plans to tackle obesity remain a little thin.

Do safe-injection sites work?

America's opioid epidemic is raging. In 2018 alone, opioid overdoses killed 47,590 Americans. But a promising remedy may be at hand. In October 2019 a federal district judge in Pennsylvania ruled that safe-injection sites – facilities where people can take drugs under the supervision of medical professionals – do not violate federal law. The "crack house statute", a provision of the 1986 Controlled Substances Act, makes it illegal to maintain a property where illicit drugs are being used. But the judge, Gerald McHugh, found that it does not apply to safe-injection sites. If Safehouse, a non-profit organisation and the defendant in the case, succeeds in opening its proposed site in Philadelphia, the facility would become America's first such clinic.

Giving addicts a place to shoot up without fear of arrest may seem peculiar to many Americans. But in Europe they are common. The first "drug-consumption room" was opened in Bern, the capital of Switzerland, in 1986 at the height of the AIDS epidemic. The aim was to contain open-air drug markets and combat diseases spread by dirty needles. Since then, dozens more have opened across the continent (by 2018, the Netherlands was leading the way, with 31 sites in 25 cities). Most offer clean needles and have medical staff on hand to treat those who have overdosed on heroin with naloxone, which temporarily reduces the drug's effect on the brain and kick-starts breathing. The best-equipped sites also provide food, showers, clothing, health care, counselling and drug-addiction treatment.

Opponents argue that such facilities give junkies a haven to feed their addiction, and that they contribute to more overdoses. In an op-ed for the *New York Times* in 2018, Rod Rosenstein, then America's deputy attorney-general, warned that safe-injection sites would expose more people to harm and destroy the communities such facilities operate in. The evidence suggests otherwise. In 2003 Canada's first safe-injection site opened in Vancouver. Since then 3.6m people have injected drugs there without any fatal overdoses.

After a drug-consumption room was opened in Barcelona, researchers estimated that the number of stray syringes found on the city's streets fell from 13,000 to 3,000 per month.

Safehouse paused its plans to open a safe-injection site in Philadelphia in February 2020, so that it can consult more widely with the local community. But other cities including New York, San Francisco and Seattle are considering similar schemes. Several states are also on board. In 2018 Jerry Brown, then California's governor, vetoed a bill that would have allowed San Francisco to open a safe-injection site. But his successor, Gavin Newsom, has said he is open to the idea. Some American politicians, it seems, are shifting their approach in the "war on drugs" from punishing offenders to reducing harm.

Have peanut allergies become more prevalent?

Food allergies have plagued humans for thousands of years. In the fifth century BC Hippocrates noted that although some people could eat their fill of cheese "without the slightest hurt ... others come off badly". The difference, he observed, "lies in the constitution of the body". Nearly all foods are capable of triggering allergic reactions in humans, and today these are more prevalent than ever, for reasons that are poorly understood. In America, as many as one in 12 children is reckoned to have a food allergy. None is more feared than that associated with the peanut. A paper by researchers at the Mayo Clinic in Minnesota found that the number of emergency-room visits by American children suffering allergic reactions to nuts, seeds and other food had tripled in ten years. Peanuts topped the list, sending nearly six in 100,000 children to hospital in 2014. More than one child in 50 is allergic to peanuts; among one-year-olds, one in 20. This figure has tripled since 2001.

Makers of packaged foods cover their products with warnings about peanuts. (Many schools and airlines now ban all nuts outright.) Allergy sufferers must monitor their diets with clinical precision. The only way to prevent severe, potentially life-threatening reactions is to avoid peanuts altogether. Anaphylaxis – a severe allergic reaction that can cause death, not least by asphyxiation or low blood pressure – is the biggest worry. Most such reactions can be treated with epinephrine, a hormone commonly known as adrenaline, but some require a rush to hospital.

This may be about to change. In September 2019 an expert advisory panel at America's Food and Drug Administration (FDA) voted to approve a new treatment for peanut allergies in children – the first of its kind. Called Palforzia, the drug seeks to treat peanut-allergy sufferers by exposing them to the very thing that could kill them. Getting the body used to the allergen, by consuming it first in tiny amounts and then in ever-larger portions, can help. Palforzia does this with pharmaceutical-grade peanut protein. A clinical trial found that after six months, more than two-thirds of allergic

Shock treatment

United States

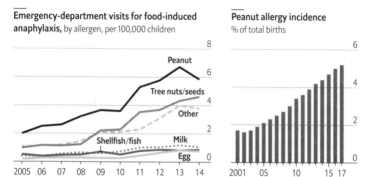

Emergency-department visits for food-induced anaphylaxis, by allergen, per 100,000 children

Peanut

Tree nuts/seeds

Other

Shellfish/fish   Milk

Egg

Peanut allergy incidence
% of total births

Sources: "National trends in emergency department visits and hospitalizations for food-induced anaphylaxis in US children", M.S. Motosue *et al., Pediatric Allergy and Immunology*, 2018; "Increased incidence and prevalence of peanut allergy in children and adolescents in the United States", J. Lieberman *et al., Annals of Asthma, Allergy & Immunology*, 2018

children could tolerate 600 milligrams of the stuff, equivalent to about two peanut kernels. The FDA approved the use of Palforzia in January 2020. But until the treatment is widely deployed, "may contain nuts" will remain a threat, not a promise.

What's the flap about chlorinated chicken?

America and Britain have started laying the groundwork for a post-Brexit trade deal. America's trade envoy, Robert Lighthizer, has called for an ambitious agreement. Agreeing to a deal will be important politically, to show that post-Brexit hopes for a "global Britain" are more than bluster. Yet many Britons already worry about what this may mean. They fear that a Britain adrift from the European Union will be in a weak negotiating position and obliged to make nasty compromises. These include opening up the NHS to foreign competition, and reducing consumer and environmental regulations. A particular bone of contention concerns chlorinated chicken. In America, after birds are slaughtered, their carcasses are washed with chemicals to manage pathogens such as salmonella and *E. coli* – a process known as "pathogen reduction treatment" (PRT). American exports of PRT-treated chicken have been rejected by the EU since 1997, and the issue remains a sore spot.

As part of any trade deal between America and Britain it seems highly likely that Britain will be required to accept PRT-treated birds. The EU argues that America's use of antimicrobial treatments is a way to compensate for poor hygiene in parts of the production process, and that rinses are used as an easy fix to clean up tainted meat. America says this criticism is unscientific and constitutes a form of protectionism, designed to shield poultry producers in the EU from imports of cheaper American chickens. There is some truth in both arguments. But it is worth noting that American regulators, who have approved a number of different kinds of antimicrobial rinse for use in poultry processing, have deemed PRT safe, and that European scientists do not seem to think there is much to worry about.

Americans eat about 150m chickens each week that have been treated with PRTs, and they have come to little harm. Britons worried about these birds should consider that they are already ingesting small amounts of disinfection by-products. According to the Adam Smith Institute, a pro-trade think-tank, chlorinated poultry would make up 0.3–1% of the disinfection by-products consumed in the typical daily diet. (Drinking water, which is also treated with chlorine, makes up 99%.) American chickens would also be far cheaper, which would benefit consumers. And nobody would be obliged to buy chlorinated chickens. Organic chicken from America is not processed with PRTs. All in all, chlorinated chicken is a paltry concern compared with the many other things trade negotiators will have on their plates.

How a stroll in the park makes you happier

"There are moments", wrote Henry David Thoreau, "when all anxiety and stated toil are becalmed in the infinite leisure and repose of nature." Thoreau, who famously spent two years living alone in a forest cabin near Walden Pond in Massachusetts, understood the restorative powers of nature. But one need not flee to the wilderness to benefit from Earth's natural beauty. Research suggests that a stroll through a neighbourhood park can boost one's mood. The greener the park, the bigger the effect.

It may seem like common sense that spending time outdoors improves your state of mind. But evidence for such a link is sparse. Studies have found that greener neighbourhoods are associated with lower levels of depression. Children who grow up around green space are less likely to develop psychiatric disorders. When asked to visit green spaces, research subjects report higher levels of well-being. And yet demonstrating an empirical relationship between nature and happiness has proved difficult.

A paper published in 2019 by researchers at the University of Vermont attempts to do this by going to the park and listening to tweets: that is, by analysing data from social-media posts. The authors compiled a list of Twitter users who had posted a tweet within the boundaries of a park or other green space in San Francisco between May and August 2016. From this list of nearly 5,000 Twitter users, the authors collected tweets published during the hours before, during and after their park visits. These tweets were analysed using the Hedonometer, a tool designed to measure the sentiment of social-media content. This tool, which is based on a database of more than 10,000 words rated on a scale from 1 (least happy) to 9 (most happy), has been used in previous academic studies and correlates with traditional survey-based measures of well-being.

The authors found that tweets published while visiting a park were about 4% "happier" than those published before or after the visit. This improvement in sentiment, the authors point out, is comparable to that observed across Twitter on Christmas Day. Park-goers became less self-centred and more positive: use of the word "me" dropped by 38%; negative words like "no", "not" and "don't" also fell. Bigger parks and parks with higher levels of greenery led to a bigger increase in tweet "happiness". Such apparent contentment lingered for at least an hour.

Exposure to nature appears to improve mental health. Yet much of the world is set to urbanise rapidly in the coming years. Today just over half of the world's population lives in cities; by 2050 the UN reckons it will be 68%. As cities grow ever more populated, green spaces may get squeezed out. "With most of the planet's population now living in cities," the authors conclude, "we must find ways to bring nature to them." Thoreau would surely agree.

What is the most dangerous drug?

Why is alcohol legal but many other intoxicants are not? That question is the subject of a report published in June 2019 by the Global Commission on Drug Policy, an independent group of 26 former presidents and other bigwigs. They conclude that, as far as the scientific evidence is concerned, current drug laws have no rhyme or reason to them. The commission blames the UN's drug classification system, which sorts some 300 psychoactive substances into "schedules" according to their harms and benefits. Some, such as morphine, have medical uses. Others, such as psilocybin (the active ingredient in magic mushrooms), are used mostly recreationally. Drugs without any apparent medical utility are automatically placed in the most dangerous category, and subjected to the strictest criminal penalties, regardless of the risk they pose.

The flaws of the UN's system have been evident for years. In 2010 a group of British drug experts ranked 20 popular intoxicating substances on 16 physical, psychological and social harms, including those done to non-users, such as crime and family breakdown. As the chart shows, alcohol came out as the most harmful, followed by heroin and crack cocaine. Psychedelic "party" drugs, including ecstasy, LSD and mushrooms, were deemed mostly benign – with harm scores less than half that of tobacco – despite being lumped with cocaine and heroin in the UN's classification system. This ranking is not without its own idiosyncrasies, many of which reflect how drugs are currently used and regulated. Alcohol's position at the top is partly the result of its widespread use, which causes greater harms to others (crack cocaine is considered the most harmful drug for the user). Drugs such as heroin, meanwhile, would be ranked lower if users could always buy an unadulterated dose, and did not have to resort to sharing needles.

Designing laws for drugs that are consistent with their dangers and benefits requires predicting how drug markets will respond. Difficult as that may be, it is the way forward, argues the Global

Paying through the nose

Britain, drug harm score (out of 100), selected drugs, 2010

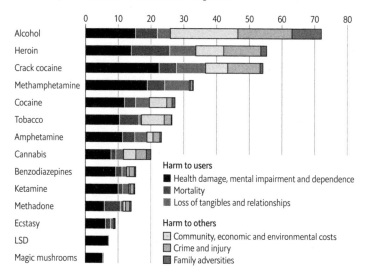

Source: "Drug harms in the UK: a multicriteria decision analysis", D.J. Nutt *et al., Lancet,* 2010

Commission. The zero-tolerance approach adopted by many governments has led to a host of social problems, including soaring prison costs and ill-health. "It is past high time to accept the fact that a society without drugs is an illusion," the report argues. Regulating drugs in a more sensible manner would make them safer – and not just for those who take them.

Do people become happier after 40?

"Life begins at 40", according to an old saying popularised by a self-help book from the 1930s. The theory goes that years of hard work are rewarded with less stress and better pay; children begin to fly the nest; and with luck, a decent period of good health remains. A quick glance at self-reported happiness across the world appears to corroborate this view.

People in their teens and early 20s start out reasonably cheerful. Gallup, a pollster, asked a representative sample of people in 158 countries to rate their life satisfaction on a scale from zero to ten. The data reported by the authors of the World Happiness Report, an academic study backed by the UN, show that happiness among people across the world aged 15 to 19 was 5.35 on average in 2016–18. A slow depression then appears to set in. By the age of 35–39 average self-reported happiness falls to 5.09 points. Once people hit 40 the satisfaction score gradually lifts. At the age of 70 an individual's self-reported happiness rises to 5.58 points, on average. On this basis happiness during a person's lifetime follows a gentle U-shape.

Life satisfaction does not follow this pattern in all countries. Self-reported happiness in former Soviet states declines markedly with a respondent's age. Among males in India it is an inverted U: happiness rises towards middle age before declining into old age. Indians are among the gloomiest people in the world, and their average life satisfaction has fallen by 1.2 points over the past decade. When Indian men reach their 70s they are among the least happy in the world, reporting average life satisfaction of just 3.6 points. By contrast women aged 70 and over in America appear to be the world's happiest group of people, with life satisfaction of some 7.5 points. The reasons for these differences are not well understood, but the idea of a U-shape has been discussed by sociologists for decades.

One difficulty is that the data provide just a snapshot, so may simply be measuring cohorts of people rather than changes in individuals' happiness as they age. By using longitudinal data,

If you're happy and you know it

Average self-reported happiness by age, 2016–18, 10=maximum

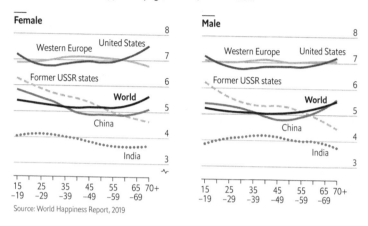

Source: World Happiness Report, 2019

which track the same people over a long period of time, several studies have tried to find out whether happiness really is U-shaped. A 2012 study of happiness among Australians, Britons and Germans between 1980 and 2010 found that after controlling for income, relationships, health and the fact that longitudinal panels may be biased, self-reported happiness was flat between the ages of 20 and 55. It then rose until the age of 75 as people enjoyed a stress-free life before declining sharply as their health deteriorated. Another study published in 2015 used the same data but employed a different methodology and found evidence for a U-shape after all. It concluded that happiness is a simple function of vitality and emotional maturity: the latter rises with age, while vitality deteriorates with age, but in concert they combine to minimise happiness at around middle age.

Children play a part, too. A working paper published by the National Bureau of Economic Research in 2019 found that children increase the happiness of European parents, especially for the first ten years. Parents become less happy, however, if having children causes them to encounter financial difficulties. It follows, then, that happiness bounces back for financially stretched parents once those children become financially independent, but decreases for those parents who enjoyed their children in financial comfort. Whether or not life begins at 40, then, seems to hinge on the matter of money and kids.

Why the road to universal health care in America is so rocky

America is the only rich country in the world that does not offer affordable health care to its entire population. "Medicare for All", an ambitious proposal to expand America's government health plan for the elderly, would change that. Every Democrat who ran for president in 2020 agreed that America's health-care system needs reform. But the debate over how to do so divided the Democratic field more than any other issue. Senators Bernie Sanders and Elizabeth Warren, the proposal's main champions, proposed the abolition of private health insurance and its replacement with a government-run "single-payer" system akin to Britain's National Health Service (NHS). More moderate candidates – Joe Biden, Amy Klobuchar and Pete Buttegieg – supported a public option, but without abolishing private health insurance. All three said they would achieve universal coverage through more incremental means, such as expanding the Affordable Care Act – better known as Obamacare.

The great attraction of Medicare for All is that it promises to provide universal coverage while eliminating nearly all insurance premiums, deductibles and out-of-pocket payments. The attention paid to health care in the Democratic primary was warranted, given that the average family's premiums on private health insurance have risen by 54% over the past decade. Building a single-payer system is also possible, as the experience of other developed countries proves.

But there are four potential snags. First, experience with frugal government-run health care elsewhere suggests that Americans may have to endure longer queues, diminished or delayed access to new therapies and a smaller selection of doctors than they are used to. Second, such comprehensive reform is likely to be disruptive. The abolition of private-health insurers could, on one estimate, eliminate 2m jobs. Many hospitals and doctors might be squeezed financially when the government slashes reimbursement rates

– possibly by 40% – from the levels paid by insurers today to the stingy amounts paid by Medicare for the same procedures.

Third, reform could be costly. Providing care for the uninsured, nearly a tenth of America's population, would not come cheap, and slashing out-of-pocket costs will encourage greater consumption by those with insurance. Studies by George Mason University and the Urban Institute, a think-tank, estimate that Medicare for All could require an additional $32trn–34trn in federal spending during its first decade. Advocates of the policy respond that such estimates ignore future cost savings, which they claim could exceed $10trn over time by curbing health-care inflation, boosting preventive care and tackling overtreatment, fraud and red tape.

What may prove more salient politically than the cost is the question of who will pay. Most universal health-care systems in the West are broadly financed, often by payroll taxes. Few are free at the point of service, as the NHS is. Ms Warren argued that the ultra-wealthy and corporations, not the middle class, should pay for Medicare for All. But her attempt to lay out such a financing plan was widely criticised and preceded a big slide in the polls. Mr Sanders, by contrast, avoided getting enmeshed in the details of how to pay for his plan. But such a massive health-care reform would require congressional approval. As long as Republicans maintain control of the Senate, Medicare for All will remain a pipe dream, no matter who sits in the White House.

Which countries have the most overweight youngsters?

Twenty years ago UNICEF, the United Nations' children's agency, took a detailed look at the diet of the world's youngsters. The story was grim: malnutrition contributed to more than half of all child deaths. The picture has since changed, in many ways for the better. Rising incomes have lifted millions out of poverty; since 1990 the burden of hunger has been cut by two-thirds. UNICEF's latest deep dive into the state of children's nutrition is again disturbing, but for a different reason. These days, children are getting either too little of the food they need, or too much of the food they do not.

The number of overweight adolescents is particularly shocking. Since the 1970s there has been a 10- to 12-fold rise in obesity among those aged 10 to 19. In poor countries, it is the relatively well-off who tend to suffer. In rich ones, it is often poorer children who carry excessive weight. In America, for example, nearly one in five youngsters in low-income households are obese, compared with just one in ten in high-income ones. Low- and middle-income countries are catching up with their richer counterparts. Disturbingly, even the youngest are affected. Since 2000, the number of overweight children under five around the world has increased by 44%.

Ballooning waistlines are often blamed on the shift towards modern diets, urbanisation and falling levels of physical activity. Economics matters, too. In many countries, the unhealthiest and most fattening foods are also the cheapest. And obesity, in turn, imposes an economic cost. Countries with lots of overweight children can expect lower levels of productivity, higher mortality and higher health-care spending on treating the maladies that come with excessive weight, such as type-2 diabetes and cardiovascular disease.

Along with children who get too many of the wrong calories, there are still those who suffer from conventional malnourishment, including children who are "stunted" (meaning they are unusually

The scale of the problem
Children and adolescents who are overweight*, 2016, %

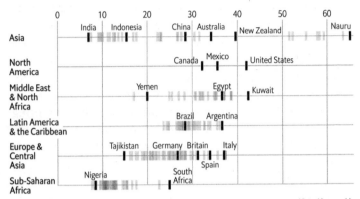

Sources: UNICEF; World Bank   *5- to 19-year-olds

short for their age) and "wasted" (they weigh too little for their height). Then there are those who suffer from "hidden hunger" – a deficiency of vitamins and other essential nutrients. Iron deficiency, for example, reduces a child's ability to learn. In total, UNICEF reckons that nearly one in three school-aged children aged 5 to 19 is overweight (18%) or underweight (11%). The world has much work to do to ensure that its children both eat well and eat healthily.

Why bats are linked to so many viruses

Which animal SARS-CoV-2 leapt from to infect human beings remains unknown. But the evidence suggests that bats were involved at some point – perhaps not as the immediate source of the virus, but probably as the reservoir from which it ultimately came. That was almost certainly true of the virus which caused the original SARS outbreak, in 2002. Though it was transmitted to people by palm civets, they probably caught it from horseshoe bats. MERS, another coronavirus, is similarly suspected of starting in bats, though the immediate source of human infection was camels. Bats are also reckoned to be behind the spread of Ebola and Marburg fevers, which are viral infections as well, though not caused by coronaviruses. And vampire bats famously carry another virus, rabies. So why are bats linked to so many viruses?

This seems to be more than just a coincidence, and has led people to ask if there is something special about bats which encourages the evolution within them of viruses predisposed to jump the species barrier and infect other sorts of animals. At the moment, the evidence is mixed.

In favour of the idea is an experiment conducted by Cara Brook of the University of California, Berkeley, and published in February 2020 in the journal *eLIFE*. This suggests a possible mechanism. Some species of bats, though not all, have unusual immune systems, in which an antiviral process known as the interferon pathway is always active, rather than only being switched on in response to infection. Dr Brook and her colleagues conducted experiments on cells from bats that have this arrangement and on others which do not (and also on cells from monkeys, for comparison). They concluded that always-on interferon pathways probably do speed up viral evolution. That would make bats more abundant sources of virulent new viruses than other groups of mammals. This mechanism does not make bat viruses more likely to jump the species barrier, but it does make them more likely to be bad news if they do.

Against the idea, however, is work by Nardus Mollentze and Daniel Streicker of the University of Glasgow published in April 2020 in *Proceedings of the National Academy of Sciences*. They found that the number of viruses which have passed to people from 11 orders of mammals and birds is pretty much proportional to the number of species in each order. Bats are the second-most diverse mammalian order, after rodents. "It is therefore not surprising," Dr Mollentze observes, "that as a group they are associated with a large number of viruses." Although bats' immune systems do indeed have the unusual features that interested Dr Brook and her colleagues, Dr Mollentze and Dr Streicker found no evidence that these caused bat-associated viruses to be more numerous, or more prone to infect people, than viruses associated with other animal groups.

This study is in line with work done specifically on coronaviruses by Tracey Goldstein of the University of California, Davis. In 2017 she and her colleagues published a piece of research which involved testing for coronaviruses in bats, rodents and primates (including people) in 20 countries in Africa, South America and Asia. Individual bat species normally had between one and five types of coronavirus. (For comparison, human beings have seven, including the newly emerged SARS-CoV-2.) Scale that up for the 1,400 different species of the animals and it means there are potentially more than 3,000 coronaviruses circulating in bats. This certainly increases the odds that bats will be responsible for generating a coronavirus dangerous to people. But only because there are so many species of them.

By the numbers: economical, with the truth

The link between wealth and road deaths

People who live in wealthy countries tend to own cars and use them often. Their cities are more spread out than those in poorer countries, and they have places to go – cinemas, restaurants, violin lessons for their children. In the poorest countries, many people live miles from a paved road, and even a bicycle is a status symbol. So you might expect that road-death rates would be highest in the rich world. The opposite is the case. With a few striking exceptions, the proportion of people who are killed on the roads each year is lowest in the wealthiest countries.

The Institute for Health Metrics and Evaluation (IHME), an American academic institute, has estimated road-death rates for every country. Some countries, like America, have good data. Others, like Somalia, do not, so the academics rely on proxy indicators and what are known as "verbal autopsies" – asking how people died. The poorest, most chaotic countries remain mysterious. The Central African Republic is thought to have an annual road-death rate of 76 per 100,000 – higher than anywhere else. The researchers are 95% confident that the true figure is between 43 and 99 per 100,000.

The data suggest that, below a certain level of income, there is not much correlation with death rates. Some upper-middle-income countries, such as the Dominican Republic or Thailand, seem to have deadlier roads than much poorer places such as Liberia. Sometimes that is because of the popularity of motorbikes – and the unpopularity of motorbike helmets. But when countries reach a GDP per head (at purchasing-power parity) of about $30,000, death rates usually start to come down. Countries above that level tend to have carefully engineered roads, diligent police, well-maintained cars and few teenage drivers.

The big exceptions to this pattern are Arab countries such as Oman, Qatar and Saudi Arabia. Though wealthy, they have high road-death rates. Officials in those countries sometimes suggest that mobile phones and wandering camels are to blame. It is more likely that their roads are deadly because people drive too fast.

Driving lesson

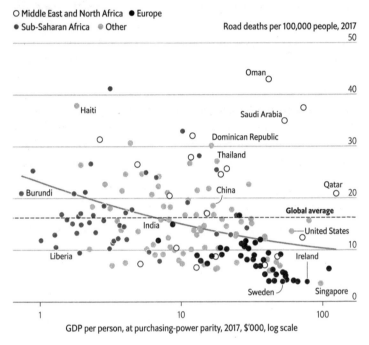

○ Middle East and North Africa ● Europe
● Sub-Saharan Africa ○ Other

Road deaths per 100,000 people, 2017

Sources: World Bank; IHME

Oman has been experimenting with "zero tolerance" speed cameras – previously, cameras would only flash at vehicles travelling more than 15km (9 miles) per hour over the speed limit. The death rate is already coming down.

Can money buy happiness?

Do a country's inhabitants get happier as it gets richer? Most governments seem to believe so, given their relentless focus on increasing GDP year by year. Reliable, long-term evidence linking wealth and happiness is, however, lacking. And measuring well-being is itself fraught with problems, since it often relies on surveys that ask participants to assess their own levels of happiness subjectively. Daniel Sgroi of the University of Warwick and Eugenio Proto of the University of Glasgow think they have an answer. By examining millions of books and newspaper articles published since 1820 in four countries (America, Britain, Germany and Italy), they have developed what they hope is an objective measure of each place's historical happiness. And their answer is that wealth does bring happiness, but some other things bring more of it.

Previous research has shown that people's underlying levels of happiness are reflected in what they say or write. Dr Sgroi and Dr Proto therefore consulted newspaper archives and Google Books, a collection of more than 8m titles that constitute around 6% of all books physically published. They searched these texts for words that had been assigned a psychological "valence" – a value representing how emotionally positive or negative a word is – while controlling for the changing meanings of words such as "gay" and "awful" (which once most commonly meant "to inspire awe"). The result is the National Valence Index, published in October 2019 in *Nature Human Behaviour*.

Placed alongside the timeline of history, the valence indices for the places under study show how changes in national happiness reflect important events. In Britain, for example, happiness fell sharply during the two world wars. It began to rise again after 1945, peaked in 1950, and then fell gradually, including through the so-called Swinging Sixties, until it reached a nadir around 1980. America's national happiness, too, fell during the world wars. It also fell in the 1860s, during and after the country's civil war. The lowest point of all came in 1975, at the end of a long decline during

It was the best of times...

National subjective well-being, derived from analysis of digitised books

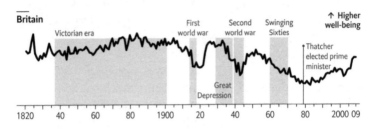

Britain

Higher well-being ↑

Victorian era · First world war · Second world war · Swinging Sixties · Thatcher elected prime minister · Great Depression

1820 · 40 · 60 · 80 · 1900 · 20 · 40 · 60 · 80 · 2000 09

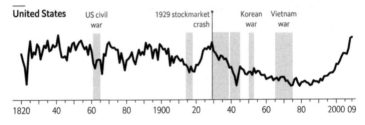

United States

US civil war · 1929 stockmarket crash · Korean war · Vietnam war

1820 · 40 · 60 · 80 · 1900 · 20 · 40 · 60 · 80 · 2000 09

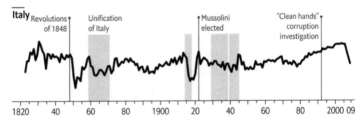

Italy Revolutions of 1848 · Unification of Italy · Mussolini elected · "Clean hands" corruption investigation

1820 · 40 · 60 · 80 · 1900 · 20 · 40 · 60 · 80 · 2000 09

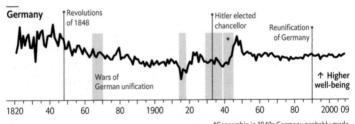

Germany Revolutions of 1848 · Hitler elected chancellor · Reunification of Germany · Wars of German unification

Higher well-being ↑

1820 · 40 · 60 · 80 · 1900 · 20 · 40 · 60 · 80 · 2000 09

*Censorship in 1940s Germany probably made its published output seem more positive

Source: "Historical analysis of national subjective wellbeing using millions of digitized books", T.T. Hills *et al., Nature Human Behaviour*, 2019

the Vietnam war, with the fall of Saigon and America's humiliating defeat.

In Germany and Italy the first world war also caused dips in happiness. By contrast, during the second world war these countries both got happier as the war continued. Initially, that might be put down to their early successes, but this can hardly explain German happiness when the Red Army was at the gates of Berlin. The researchers hypothesise that what is being measured here is the result of propaganda and censorship, rather than honest opinion. But they cannot prove this. Earlier in Italian history, though, there was a clear and explicable crash in happiness in 1848, with the failure of revolutions intended to unite what were then half a dozen disparate states into a single nation. Surprisingly, however, successful unification in the 1860s also saw a fall in happiness.

As to wealth, the steady economic progress of the Victorian period matches a steady increase in British happiness, as did the economic boom of the 1920s, which also lifted American spirits. Both countries' spirits fell again in the Depression that followed the stockmarket crash of 1929. After the lows of the 1970s, though, happiness in both has been on the rise ever since.

Overall, then, Dr Sgroi and Dr Proto found that happiness does vary with GDP. But the effect of health (measured by life expectancy), which does not have the episodic quality of booms, busts and armed conflict, is larger, even when the tendency of wealth to improve health is taken into account. A one-year increase in longevity, for example, has the same effect on national happiness as a 4.3% increase in GDP. And, as the grand historical sweep suggests, it is warfare that causes the biggest drops in happiness. On average it takes a 30% increase in GDP to raise happiness by the amount that a year of war causes it to fall. The upshot appears to be that, although increasing national income is important to happiness, it is not as important as ensuring the population is healthy and avoiding conflict.

Does cutting taxes really raise revenues?

Rarely has a dinner-table scribbling created such a legacy. In 1974 Arthur Laffer, an economist, sketched a simple diagram on the back of a napkin to illustrate a truism of tax policy. Set income-tax rates to zero and governments will not collect any revenue. Set them to 100%, and they will also collect nothing because people will have little incentive to work. Somewhere in between lies a sweet spot where government revenues are maximised. From this simple proof, it follows that when tax rates are very high, it might be possible both to lower tax rates and raise revenues. Tax cuts might thus pay for themselves, and more.

Mr Laffer's scribbling caught on. Some 45 years later some 15,000 journal articles mention the "Laffer curve" in their title. In June 2019 President Donald Trump awarded the Presidential Medal of Freedom, America's highest civilian honour, to Mr Laffer – an adviser to his 2016 presidential campaign and co-author of the book *Trumponomics*. In its announcement of the event, the White House described Mr Laffer as "one of the most influential economists in American history".

Budget hawks might disagree. Supply-side economists have long used the Laffer curve to justify tax cuts, including those introduced by Ronald Reagan in 1981 and George W. Bush in 2001. Both resulted in lower, rather than higher, revenues. In December 2017 Mr Trump's administration cut income taxes across the board, and slashed the corporate-tax rate from 35% to 21%. At the time, Steven Mnuchin, America's treasury secretary, argued that the plan would "pay for itself" and even "pay down debt". But the promised revenues failed to materialise. Federal tax revenues actually fell in 2018. The Congressional Budget Office, a government watchdog, estimated in 2019 that the national debt would hit 95% of GDP by 2027, up from 89% in 2017, before the tax cuts.

America is not the only country that appears to be on the wrong side of Mr Laffer's curve. A paper published in 2017 by Jacob Lundberg, an economist at Timbro, a Swedish free-market

Finding the sweet spot

Estimated Laffer curve for the top marginal income-tax rate, 2017

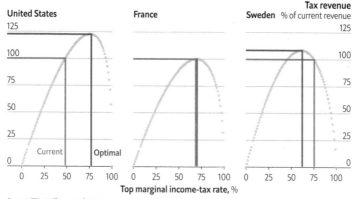

Source: "The Laffer curve for high incomes", J. Lundberg, LIS working paper, 2017

think-tank, estimates Laffer curves for 27 OECD countries. Using data on Sweden's income distribution and assumptions about how taxpayers respond to different tax rates, Mr Lundberg found that, even though five countries in his sample have top income-tax rates that exceed their revenue-maximising levels, only Sweden could meaningfully boost revenue by cutting tax rates on high-income earners. Most countries, in other words, appear to have set their highest tax rates at or below the optimal rate suggested by the Laffer curve. This may explain why many economists are so critical of Mr Laffer's supply-side policies. In 2012 the Initiative on Global Markets, a research centre at the University of Chicago's Booth School of Business, asked a panel of 40 economic experts whether a cut in income-tax rates in America would raise enough revenue to pay for itself in five years. Not one of them said it would. Richard Thaler, winner of the 2018 Nobel prize in economics, responded simply "That's a Laffer!"

What satellite data reveal about North Korea's economy

Viewed from space at night, North Korea looks like an image of a black hole: an abyss, ringed by the brilliant glow of South Korea, China and Russia, from which nothing can escape. But the Hermit Kingdom does emit a bit of light, which orbiting satellites detect. And nocturnal luminosity is one of the few reliable sources of information about the country. It implies that North Korea's economy is poorer, more volatile and more vulnerable to weather than formerly thought.

Night lights are a strong proxy for economic activity. A paper by the IMF found that they explain 44% of the variation in countries' GDP per person – as close a tie as that between a person's height and hand size. In places where records are poor or manipulated, night lights offer an alternative measure of output. One study found that among countries with similar luminosity, autocracies reported GDP growth 15–30% higher than democracies did.

Nowhere are good economic data rarer than in North Korea. The most detailed numbers come from South Korea's central bank, which derives them from figures on production volumes of various goods. When adjusted for the cost of living in a developing Asian economy, the bank's 2019 estimate of North Korea's annual GDP per person suggested that it was enough to buy goods and services that would cost $2,500 in America. The picture painted by night lights, however, is even grimmer. In 2013 a group of scholars compared luminosity and GDP within rural China, obtaining an equation to estimate economic output from light. A paper by World Data Lab, a startup, and a team of researchers applies this formula to North Korea. It yields a standard of living that would cost $1,400 a year in America, making North Korea one of the world's ten poorest countries.

The data also suggest that the economy has been unusually volatile. Between 2013 and 2015 luminosity fell by 40%. That implies a 12% reduction in GDP, including 19% in the region of the capital, Pyongyang. Since 2016, however, the country has brightened again. International sanctions are unlikely to have produced this darkening. They were made stricter in 2016–17, just as luminosity rose. A drop in the prices of North Korean exports, like coal, may have played a part.

But the main cause was probably weather. North Korea relies on hydropower, and in 2015 it was parched by a drought. The Bank of Korea also reckons that electricity, gas and water output fell by 13% in 2015. The economy may not have shrunk as much as the dimming suggests. Recessions caused by power cuts could disproportionately reduce lighting. Many North Koreans own solar panels, which power daytime activity not shown in night lights. And state buildings, whose illumination is a political choice, make up much of the capital's glow. As with physics inside a black hole, no one knows what economic laws apply within North Korea's eerie silhouette. Nonetheless, a 40% drop in luminosity indicates a serious recession. And in 2019 the government admitted publicly that heatwaves, floods and drought had caused a dire food shortfall. The regime appears better prepared to weather trade sanctions than the wrath of nature.

Will American millennials be as rich as they think?

More than half of American millennials, the generation of people born between 1981 and 1996, believe that they will one day be millionaires; one in five think they will get there by the age of 40. These are the findings from a survey conducted in 2018 by TD Ameritrade, a financial-services company. But a working paper published in 2019 by the Brookings Institution, a think-tank, offers a sobering antidote to this youthful optimism. It finds that millennials are less wealthy than people of a similar age were in any year from 1989 to 2007. The economic crisis of 2008–09 hit millennials particularly hard. Median household wealth in 2016 for 20- to 35-year-olds was about 25% lower than it was for the similar-aged cohort in 2007.

American millennials are comparatively poor because many of them came of age during the financial crisis, when demand for labour was low and borrowing money became harder. The subsequent recovery was slow, which further reduced millennials' long-term earning potential. A paper by the Federal Reserve, published in 2018, found that millennial household incomes were 11% lower than they were for people in Generation X (defined as those born between the mid-1960s and 1981) at a comparable age; they were 14% lower than for baby-boomers at the same point in their lives. A growing number of young people have taken on debt to finance their studies. And because real wages have not kept up with inflation, the cost of living has risen.

Worse still, the Brookings paper reports that young people's prospects for accumulating wealth in old age are grim. Millennials do more freelance and part-time work than other generations did, which makes it more difficult to obtain an employer-provided pension. Only 55% of this generation have access to retirement plans, compared with 77% of Generation X and 80% of baby-boomers. Moreover, those who do have employer pensions are more likely to have defined-contribution pensions than defined-benefit ones, meaning that they bear the risk if investment returns disappoint. And as America seeks to plug its long-term fiscal shortfalls, millennials will have to bear the burden of any future cuts to Social Security and Medicare. All this helps explain why the share of Americans aged 25 to 34 who are living with their parents has increased from 10% in 2000 to about 15% in 2019. That is not quite the high life millennials imagined.

But all is not lost. Millennials are living longer and are the best-educated generation in history. Taken together, this could yet mean that the youngest millennials, who were less scarred by the financial crisis, could contribute towards their retirement pots for longer. Then there is mum and dad. Even if they do not become millionaires, millennials will one day inherit from their parents, and that may help redress their relative poverty.

Why Indians are falling out of love with gold

The Hindu festival of Akshaya Tritiya, celebrated in late April or early May, is considered an auspicious time to buy gold. Queues outside Indian jewellery stores become so long that makeshift tents are set up to accommodate the rush. Cashiers hand-count wads of banknotes in conditions as noisy as those in a busy fast-food restaurant. Salesmen cater to a remarkable level of demand. As a group, Indians buy more gold than anyone apart from the Chinese (who have occupied the top spot since 2014). Collectively, Indian households are reckoned to have a stockpile of gold worth $800bn. Yet the Indian market is not as healthy as it was. Purchases of the metal have fallen by around a fifth since their peak in 2010. Why is gold losing its sheen?

Start with changing tastes and preferences. Around a third of Indians are 18 to 35 years old. They often prefer to spend their money on electronic gadgets, purchased in monthly instalments with zero interest rates, rather than jewellery. In 2017 consumer electronics toppled gold as the second-biggest contributor to India's national import bill, behind oil. Moreover, the tastes of those who buy gold appear to be changing. Heavy jewellery has given way to lightweight designs, sometimes with lesser caratage. "Gold is no longer a sign of wealth, but of fashion," admits one customer at a jewellery store in Mumbai.

Nor is gold still the go-to investment option for those whose money lies outside the formal financial system. In 2014 a state-sponsored programme opened millions of bank accounts. Mutual funds have returned 12.5% annually in the last decade. The Sensex stockmarket index gained around 60% between 2014 and 2019. In that period, the price of gold rose, in rupee terms, by just 7% from a high base, a far cry from the 12 years until 2012 when it rose by more than 500%. Its value as a hedge against inflation, at 3%, has diminished too.

India's government has long tried to wean citizens off gold, almost all of which the country imports, contributing to the current-account deficit. Since 2012 officials have raised quotas on gold imports five-fold to 10%, but have been wary of increasing the rate higher, lest they push the trade underground. In 2018 authorities seized 66kg of gold bars, worth $3m, hidden in four cars. Bootleggers will continue to seek creative ways to beat the system. But if consumers are reconsidering their love affair with gold, the government will not try to rekindle the passion.

How starting work during a recession affects workers' later lives

Timing is everything. This is especially true in the labour market. Workers who start looking for a job during a recession earn significantly less than their timelier counterparts. This wage penalty can last for years – a phenomenon economists call wage "scarring". Until recently, it was assumed that such scars were mainly economic, affecting workers' employment, income and wealth. But research by Hannes Schwandt of Northwestern University and Till von Wachter of the University of California, Los Angeles, suggests that economic downturns can have other long-lasting effects.

Using data on the roughly 4m Americans who entered the workforce shortly before, during and after the 1982 recession – when unemployment reached almost 11% – the authors measured how the downturn affected those people's health and mortality many years later. On joining the labour force, they faced a national unemployment rate 3.9 percentage points higher than that before the onset of recession. That was associated, the authors found, with a reduction in their life expectancy of six to nine months. The additional deaths were from causes linked to unhealthy behaviour, including heart disease, lung cancer, liver disease and drug poisoning.

Starting work during the recession also damaged marriages. People who entered the labour force around 1982 were more likely to get divorced (their split-up rates were about 3.5% above the average). By middle age, they were also roughly 3–4% less likely to have children. Downturns are not death sentences for new workers. But these findings reveal some of the unforeseen consequences of fluctuations in the business cycle.

How the property market is biased against single women

Women's rights advocates routinely lament the gap between men's and women's wages. But the gender gap in wealth may be just as troubling. According to the Boston Consulting Group, a consultancy, in 2015 women held just 30% of all global private wealth. The Survey of Consumer Finances, a poll of American households conducted by the Federal Reserve, shows that among single 60-year-olds, men are about twice as rich as women.

According to a recent study, some of this disparity can be explained by differences in how men and women buy and sell property. Using data on 9m housing transactions carried out in America between 1991 and 2017, Paul Goldsmith-Pinkham and Kelly Shue of the Yale School of Management found that, on average, single women pay about 2% more than their male counterparts for houses, and sell them for 2% less. Given that Americans move house an average of 11 times during their lives, this disadvantage can mount up. The authors reckon that the typical single woman loses about $1,600 in housing wealth every year as a result. What is behind the housing gender gap?

Some of it can be explained by market factors: women are more prone to buying in less promising markets and at inauspicious times. Quite why is unclear, but it may be that women are more risk-averse and so, for example, are more likely than men to sell when markets start to fall, rather than riding out the turbulence. But the authors find that the biggest reason why women lose out lies in negotiations over price. Women are less likely to bargain down a home's list price when buying, and tend to undervalue their own home when selling. As a result, the highest-priced home sales consistently occur when a man is selling to a woman; the lowest-priced ones, when a woman is selling to a man.

The authors are careful to note that this does not mean that women are necessarily less competent negotiators. Discrimination may play a significant role. In a study published in 2015, subjects

Buy high, sell low

United States, gender gap in housing market sales*, %

Trend — 95% confidence interval

Purchase price

↑ Single women buy houses for about 2% more than men

Years since home sale

Sale price

↓ And sell them for 2% less

Years since home sale

Source: "The gender gap in housing returns", P. Goldsmith-Pinkham and K. Shue, National Bureau of Economic Research, working paper, 2020

*Property listings across the US between 1991 and 2017

were asked to haggle with a car salesman. Even though all the car-buyers used the same script, the women were consistently offered worse deals. New home-buying technologies such as "i-Buying", where firms use algorithms to value properties and make initial offers, could help narrow the gender gap in housing wealth. Until then, women can expect their retirement years to be a little less golden.

How some fish pay others rent

Tenants who don't pay the rent are a bane of landlords everywhere. And landlords who use heavy tactics to enforce payment are similarly a bane of tenants. Nor are these problems confined to human beings. Property-owning cichlid fish seem as ruthless about receiving what they are owed as any 19th-century tenement holder in the Lower East Side of New York.

The fish in question, *Neolamprologus pulcher*, inhabit Lake Tanganyika in East Africa. They are co-operative breeders, meaning that dominant individuals do the breeding and subordinates assist in various ways, in exchange for immediate survival-enhancing benefits that may lead to the ultimate prize of becoming dominant themselves. In the case of *N. pulcher* the main benefit is having somewhere to live. Dwellings, in the form of shelters dug out from sand under rocks, are controlled by dominant pairs. These dominant fish permit subordinates to share their accommodation, and those subordinates pay for the privilege by keeping the property in good repair and defending the dominants' eggs and fry against predators.

Though co-operative breeding by vertebrates has evolved several times (famous examples include the meerkat mongooses of Southern Africa and the scrub jays of Florida), the question of how rental payments are enforced has never been definitively settled. The presumption is that dominants punish subordinate defaulters. But it is hard to prove, by observing wild animals, that this is what is happening. What was needed to clear up the point was an experiment. And fish are easier to experiment on than mongooses or jays. Jan Naef and Michael Taborsky of the University of Bern, in Switzerland, therefore acquired 96 specimens of *N. pulcher* and created ménages of a pair of dominant landlords and a subordinate tenant in sand-bottomed aquaria.

Left alone, the fish behaved much as they would have done in the wild, with the tenant doing the grunt work of maintaining the hollows in the sand, and good relations pertaining between all. However, when the researchers prevented a tenant from fulfilling its duties for a while, by trapping it behind a partition inserted into the aquarium for that purpose, things changed. When the partition was removed, the landlords attacked it, and it showed a big increase in submissive behaviour for several minutes before things returned to normal.

Whether similar treatment would be meted out for a failure to defend the landlords' eggs has yet to be determined. When prevented by a partition from driving away predators, tenants were not subsequently punished with aggression from landlords – but since there were no eggs to defend at the time, that may not have been part of the contract. The predators in question, a species called *Telmatochromis vittatus*, are not a threat to adult specimens of *N. pulcher*, only to eggs and fry. It is nevertheless clear from Dr Naef's and Dr Taborsky's experiment that, for cichlids at least, the rent must be paid in a timely fashion, or punishment will be faced.

How shifts in global trade explain the rise of urban coyotes

The attacker sprang from the tall grass in a lakefront park, leaving a five-year-old victim terrified, blood streaming from his head. After the boy was taken to hospital, a hunt ensued. Helicopters, police and specialist trackers fanned out across a Chicago neighbourhood. A man appeared at a hospital saying he, too, had been bitten. Two nearby schools were locked down for a day. Eventually a suspect – a brindle coyote with puppy-dog eyes – was apprehended behind a theatre.

The incident excited much of Chicago. Although coyote attacks on humans are rare, the animals have become an increasingly common part of urban American life. Once mostly found west of the Mississippi, they have spread east. Coyotes have settled in almost every urban area in the country, including New York City. There are few reliable estimates of the national population, but more than 400,000 are killed by hunters each year. Survivors roam an ever-larger territory.

In Chicago, coyote sightings have become routine, especially in the past decade. Stan Gehrt, a professor of wildlife ecology at Ohio State University, launched a study of the animals two decades ago after they began showing up in sizeable numbers. "Before then, not much research had been done into urban coyotes. We didn't know what it meant," he says. The population has soared. Depending on whether the count includes cubs, Mr Gehrt conservatively estimates that between 2,000 and 4,000 coyotes live in the city.

What lies behind this boom? The loss of deciduous forests and wolves (which hunted coyotes) are long-term factors. Federal efforts to poison the animal were scaled back in the 1970s because of concerns over the dangers of releasing toxins haphazardly into the environment. But Mr Gehrt also points to a shift in global trade. Hunters and trappers continue to kill coyotes. A pelt can sell for as much as $100, to be used as trim or linings for winter coats, including Canada Goose jackets. But overall demand for American furs from Chinese, Russian and other European buyers has slumped in recent years. With fur unfashionable, sales down and "trapping animals not as acceptable as before", rural areas have become "saturated" with the animal, Mr Gehrt says. Today, as cubs mature and seek their own territories, many have been pushed into cities.

Coyotes can be troublesome. They eat pet cats and small dogs. But on balance they are benign. They mostly eat fruit and other wild species, including pests that flourish in cities, such as rats, rabbits, woodchucks, young Canada geese and the fawns of white-tailed deer. Keeping these populations in check is a welcome public service. Predatory attacks on humans are rare. Just one American – a toddler snatched from a garden in Los Angeles in 1981 – has been reported killed by a coyote in the past four decades. Public anxiety about the spread of a large predator is understandable, but dogs are a much greater menace. They kill around 50 people and send thousands to hospital each year in America. Deer, too, appear cute but cause traffic accidents that kill more than 200 Americans a year. Coyotes may seem less docile, but they are much less deadly.

Green scene: environmental matters

More countries are banning plastic bags, but does it help?

According to the United Nations Environment Programme (UNEP), up to 5trn plastic bags are consumed each year. Disposed of improperly, they can clog waterways, choke marine life and provide a breeding-ground for malaria-carrying mosquitoes. When dumped in landfills, they can take centuries to decompose.

Plenty of governments have decided that enough is enough. More than 90 countries have banned single-use plastic bags, from Tanzania to New Zealand. Another 36 regulate them with levies and fees. Bans are particularly widespread in Africa. This is partly because relatively low waste-collection and recycling rates make the problem of waste plastic more visible, partly because Africa exports very little plastic and lacks a strong industry lobby.

The resulting international patchwork of laws has lots of loopholes. Many countries regulate just one part of the plastic-bag lifecycle, such as manufacture, distribution or disposal. The most common approach is to charge shoppers at the till. Although

Paying with plastic
Plastic-bag bans
July 2019 ■ Full ban ■ Partial ban ■ Ban under consideration ■ No ban ▨ No data

Source: UNEP

this reduces local demand for bags, it does not stop them being exported. At least 25 countries with bans – including Panama – have exemptions for perishable foods or medicines.

Some environmentalists reckon that policymakers should in any case focus their efforts elsewhere. Plastic pollution is hard to miss, but its effects are small compared with global warming or biodiversity loss. The alternatives to plastic are pretty rubbish, too. For a cotton tote bag to generate less greenhouse-gas emissions than a throwaway plastic one, it has to be used 131 times.

How to design monsoon-proof buildings

Communities on the Ganges delta in Bangladesh have lived between land and water for centuries. Most of the country is less than five metres above sea level; monsoon season lasts for four months, and it brings 80% of the annual rainfall (between 2,000 and 3,000 millimetres on average). Here, when the waters subside, buildings are erected quickly from wooden frames and corrugated metal sheets. If an area becomes uninhabitable, the structures can be dismantled and rebuilt with the same layout. Flooding will become even more frequent as the effects of climate change intensify. Flash floods are increasingly violent and tropical storms heavier. According to the Natural Resources Defense Council, a charity, by 2050 rising sea levels will have submerged 17% of Bangladesh and displaced roughly 20m people. The drier north-western regions, meanwhile, are at risk of drought.

Good design is essential if these challenges are to be addressed. The solutions are often straightforward. Since 2005 MTA, Marina Tabassum's architectural practice in Dhaka, the country's capital, has used low-cost, sustainable substances in its designs. Local materials such as teak and red brick help to create *jalees* (lattices) and *beras* (perforated screens), which provide cheap shading, shelter and ventilation. The Bait Ur Rouf Mosque, built in 2012, sits on a raised plinth to protect it from floodwater. The idea is to form buildings ideally suited to their environment, which almost grow from the site, says Ms Tabassum. She has also directed *Inheriting Wetness*, a documentary film in which she reflects on the idea of land ownership amid the "continuous interplay of erosion and accretion – a unique phenomenon that has long shaped the lives of Bengalis".

Rafiq Azam, the founder of Shatotto Architects, is working on more than 20 projects in Dhaka, revitalising abandoned public parks and waterways infested with dengue fever. "Almost all the green space in Old Dhaka plays host to vagrants and illegal activities," he says. "Our research led us to ask: why are these spaces not working?

Why are they vandalised? What can we do to protect them from prolonged monsoon and drought?" His design for the Shahid Abdul Alim playground offers some answers. The 1.3-acre site, an illegally occupied field-cum-parking lot in Old Dhaka, has been turned into playing fields and a football pitch. Walls and fences that gave shelter to unlawful shops and squatters were removed, allowing the park to be completely open. Flooding was alleviated by planting trees and collecting rainwater. Mr Azam enlisted local children to plant a mix of greenery; he added an underground trench able to hold 500,000 litres of rainwater, which is then saved for drier periods.

West of Dhaka, on the flood plains of South Kanarchor, Saif Ul Haque Sthapati, another architectural practice, has created an "amphibious structure" for an area which is under three metres of water for several months of the year. The Arcadia Education Project – which houses a pre-school, a hostel for single women and a nursery – is anchored using posts drilled into a brick, earth and sandbag foundation, and sits on the ground or floats depending on the water level. The building is mostly made from different types of local bamboo, which was floated along the river to the site. A substance made from boiled *gaab* fruit was used to waterproof the roof; most joints were tied with rope rather than steel wire to help stave off corrosion.

Dhaka, one of the world's fastest-growing megacities, must reckon with the difficulties of a tropical monsoon climate. Unfortunately, it is in the grip of developers who favour expensive, inefficient concrete-and-glass towers, studded with air-conditioning units, over traditional techniques and local materials. "The challenge is how to raise the standard of living in Bangladesh to match our own without the carbon wastefulness," says Peter Clegg, a founding partner of Feilden Clegg Bradley Studios, a British architecture firm. These buildings provide a blueprint, not just for Dhaka, but for other countries facing floods and monsoons of increasing severity.

How winemakers are responding to climate change

Galileo is said to have described wine as "sunlight, held together by water". Today's winemakers can only agree – at their own expense. Wine grapes are highly sensitive to climate. Too much heat and they accumulate excess sugar, producing overly alcoholic and flabby wines; not enough and the fruit turns into tart, acidic liquor. That is why most wine regions are in areas where average temperatures fall between 12°C and 22°C during the growing season (April to October in the northern hemisphere; October to April in the southern). These lie at latitudes of 30° to 50°. As the planet warms up, however, those bands are moving towards the poles. One study reckons that the northern frontier of vine cultivation in Europe could advance by 20–60km each decade between now and 2050.

This has led some scientists to predict the extinction of wines that are nearly synonymous with the liquid itself, such as Burgundy and Bordeaux. In contrast, those who tend to see glasses as half-full expect a new wave of *grands crus* to emerge from previously unlikely terroirs such as Sussex and Scandinavia. Many of today's top estates are already under pressure. Vintners are harvesting their grapes three weeks earlier than they did the 1960s. More of them are forced to harvest at night, to ensure the heat of summer days does not cause grapes to oxidise. Canadian producers are planting vines farther and farther north. Argentina's cellar masters are venturing as far south as Patagonia. And in Chile, where wine regions are named after valleys, growers are heading for the country's cooler hills.

A warmer climate is welcome news for northern European winemakers. But a warmer Denmark might also be a wetter one. Rain is helpful in winter and early in the season, but too much of it in the summer or early autumn results in watery grapes and a weak vintage. Excessive humidity can also bring disease, fungus and pests. Climate change brings other risks too. Vineyards at higher latitudes may be more vulnerable. In 2014 the polar vortex – a huge area of cold air around the North Pole that drifted south – wiped out entire vineyards in Ontario and New York state.

The weather will also become harder to predict. In recent decades extreme temperatures have become more frequent in wine regions, according to a study released in July 2019. Vines are being more exposed to frost in spring and heatwaves in summer. They are also seeing fewer days without rain, even in supposedly dry regions.

Both climate change and the industry's efforts to adapt make it hard to guess which regions will be cultivated – or culled – by 2050. Insiders believe Bordeaux vintners have ways of mitigating climate change's consequences if average global temperatures do not rise to more than 2°C above pre-industrial levels. These tend not to be particularly high-tech: shade netting helps protect grapes from fiercer sunshine; training vines higher puts them farther from rocky soils, which tend to radiate heat at night. If temperatures rise further, winemakers will have to try more drastic interventions, and change the practices of centuries. They could shift to grape varieties that are better suited to warmer climates. Bordeaux's winemakers, who typically lean towards Cabernet Sauvignon and Merlot, are testing out varietals from Portugal's torrid Douro valley. They might not be over a barrel just yet.

How much does giving up meat help the environment?

It is no secret that steaks and chops are delicious. But guzzling them incurs high costs for both carnivorous humans and the planet. Over half of adults in both America and Britain say they want to reduce their meat consumption, according to Mintel, a market-research firm. Whether they will is a different matter. The amount of meat that Americans and Britons consume per day has risen by 10% since 1970, according to figures from the UN's Food and Agriculture Organisation.

People who want to eat less meat, but who can't quite bring themselves to exchange burgers for beans, might take inspiration from two academic papers. A study published in November 2019 by scientists at the University of Oxford and the University of Minnesota estimates both the medical and environmental burdens of having an extra serving per day of various food types. The health findings were sobering. Compared with a typical Western adult of the same age who eats an average diet, a person who guzzles an additional 50g of processed red meat (about two rashers of bacon) per day has a 41% higher chance of dying in a given year.

Meat has an even starker impact on the environment. Compared with a 100g portion of vegetables – the standard serving size considered in academic papers – a 50g chunk of red meat is associated with at least 20 times as much greenhouse-gas emitted and 100 times as much land use. Averaged across all the ecological indicators the authors used, red meat was about 35 times as damaging as a bowl of greens. However, a newly converted vegetarian who replaces every 50g of beef she usually eats with 100g of kale would soon be famished. A standard portion of greens contains far fewer calories than a slab of meat. So an aspiring herbivore would have to eat more servings of salad than the number of burgers she has forsaken.

In 2019 a group of academics, based mainly at Johns Hopkins University, simulated the environmental effects of such

High-steak diets

Health and environmental impact
of one extra serving per day

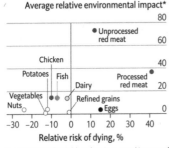

Average relative environmental impact*

United States, greenhouse-gas footprint
'000kg of CO_2 equivalent per person per year

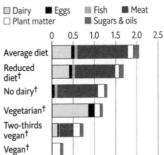

Sources: "Multiple health and environmental impacts of foods", M.A. Clark *et al.*,
PNAS, 2019; "Country-specific dietary shifts to mitigate climate and water crises",
B.F. Kim *et al.*, *Global Environmental Change*, 2020

*Vegetables=1
†Simulated diet, to reach
2,300 calories per day

substitutions. They used consumption and trading data from 140 countries to estimate which foodstuffs people might switch to in order to help the planet, and came up with several hypothetical diet plans. These would allow people to achieve the recommended amounts of energy and protein in various ways.

Giving up meat makes a big difference. By becoming a vegetarian, an American who eats 2,300 calories of a typical mix of foods can knock 30% off their annual greenhouse-gas emissions associated with food. But dairy products, produced by methane-emitting cows, also have a sizeable impact. Indeed, such is the footprint of dairy products that going vegan for two-thirds of meals, but still indulging in animal products in one-third, reduces emissions by nearly 60%. A vegan diet, which excludes both meat and dairy products, is greenest of all, reducing food-related emissions by 85%. But being a part-time vegan is, it seems, better for the planet than being a full-time vegetarian.

Why trains are not always as green as they seem

Greta Thunberg, a Swedish campaigner for action against climate change, has done much to publicise Sweden's *flygskam* ("flight-shame") movement, which encourages people to travel on trains instead of planes to reduce carbon emissions. Ms Thunberg herself shuns air travel. In August 2019 she travelled from Britain to New York by sailboat to attend a climate conference at the United Nations, saving an estimated 1.8 tonnes of carbon dioxide emissions produced by an economy-class passenger on a transatlantic return flight. A train was not an option for that voyage, but normally Ms Thunberg travels by train as much as she can.

Replacing a plane ride with a journey on an electric train can cut emissions. Eurostar, an operator of express trains through the Channel Tunnel, estimates that taking the train from London to Paris reduces carbon emissions by more than 90% per economy-class passenger compared with flying. That is because France and Britain generate more than half of their electricity from renewable sources or nuclear power plants.

But on some rail lines in countries that use dirtier diesel trains, or trains powered by electricity generated using fossil fuels, the emissions produced per passenger mile can exceed those produced by flying. One study published in 2009 by Mikhail Chester and Arpad Horvath of the University of California, Berkeley, found that passenger travel on the Boston light rail, an electric commuter train in America, produced as much or even more in emissions per passenger mile than travel on a jetliner. This was, in part, because the researchers took into account the "full life-cycle" emissions associated with building and maintaining vehicles and their infrastructure. For trains, that includes rolling stock and rails; air travel, by comparison, requires relatively little infrastructure per mile travelled. Another factor was that, a decade ago, 82% of electricity in Massachusetts was generated by burning fossil fuels. So trains are not always as green as they seem. Such complexities mean the only sure-fire way to cut your carbon emissions from travel, it would appear, is to stay at home.

How air pollution can ruin schoolchildren's lives

As part of a "public-health emergency" declared in November 2019 in Delhi, millions of face masks were distributed to children, and schools were shut down for several days. The cause was not a viral outbreak, but polluted air, which Delhi's chief minister says had turned the city into a "gas chamber". The measures were severe but not unusual. Schools in other countries around the world – in Thailand and Malaysia, Mexico and America – have also cancelled classes on bad-air days. Air pollution does indeed do terrible things to schoolchildren.

Globally, says the World Health Organisation, more than 90% of children under 15 breathe air that puts their health at serious risk. The young are especially susceptible, because their lungs are still developing and they breathe more quickly than adults, so they take in more pollutants relative to their body weight. A British study found that on school-runs young children were exposed to 30% more pollutants than the adults accompanying them, because their height put them closer to exhaust pipes. One of the most common ailments that results is asthma. Poorer children are even more vulnerable, because their schools tend to be near busy roads.

Children's brains are also at risk, and not because pollution forces them to stay at home: teachers in Malaysia and China were early adopters of online tools that allow them to instruct students remotely when smog keeps them away from school. (Besides, research in 2014 by the Harvard Kennedy School into the effect of shutting schools because of snow found that missing a few days did not appear to impair learning.) Much more dangerous is the toll that pollution takes on cognitive development and mental health. Research, also conducted in 2014, found that air pollution harmed Israeli students' exam performance. A study in Cincinnati, Ohio, showed an increase in pollution to be correlated with a higher number of psychiatric-hospital visits by children troubled by anxiety and suicidal thoughts. Even very young students are aware of the pollution problem: in one survey, 45% of British pupils aged 4 to 11 said they were worried about air quality. Such "eco-anxiety" is the reason that some American school boards are riven by disagreements between environmentalists, who maintain that children need to understand climate change, and administrators who say studying it will traumatise them.

Clean-air campaigners have tried to stem the damage. In Britain, for example, they have encouraged student pick-ups and drop-offs on foot or by bicycle, recommended the imposition of no-car zones around schools in Birmingham, and placed hedges between roads and playgrounds in Sheffield. Such measures are no substitute for bigger changes to tackle pollution at its source through tougher regulation, though. If trends persist, warns the OECD, a club of mostly rich countries, air pollution will cut 1% from global GDP by 2060, in large part from reduced agricultural yields, lower worker productivity and higher health costs. Apart from choking on the fumes, today's schoolchildren can look forward to bearing those burdens, too.

Why shrimps can be worse for the environment than beef

For a long time, beef has been a target of environmentalists because of cattle farming's contribution to global warming. But what about humble shrimp and prawns? They may seem, well, shrimpy when compared with cows, but it turns out that the tasty decapods can be just as big an environmental problem. The issue is not so much their life cycle: shrimp (as statisticians refer to all commonly eaten species collectively) do not belch planet-cooking methane the way cows do. But shrimp farms tend to occupy coastal land that used to be covered in mangroves. Draining mangrove swamps to make way for aquaculture is even more harmful to the atmosphere than felling rainforests to provide pasture for cattle. A study conducted in 2017 by the Centre for International Forestry Research (CIFOR) found that in both cases, by far the biggest contribution to the carbon footprint of the resulting shrimp or beef came from the clearing of the land. As a result, CIFOR concluded, a kilogram of farmed shrimp was responsible for almost four times the greenhouse-gas emissions of a kilogram of beef.

Eating wild shrimp is not much better: catches are declining around the world as a result of overfishing. Trawlers can pull as much as 20kg of by-catch from the sea for every kilo of shrimp. And reports abound of the appalling treatment of workers on shrimp-fishing vessels, including human-trafficking and child labour. When United Nations investigators interviewed a sample of Cambodians who had escaped modern slavery on Thai fishing boats, 59% of them reported seeing fellow crew-members murdered by the captain.

Most of the world's shrimp and prawns come from Asia. The continent accounts for 85% of the farmed sort and 74% of the wild catch. Global sales were around $45bn in 2018 and are thought to be growing by about 5% a year. But the industry is controversial, not just because of its part in global warming. Razing mangroves also leaves coastal regions vulnerable to flooding. Many shrimp farms are unsanitary; ponds often have to be abandoned after a few years because of problems with disease and pollution.

All this has given one Singaporean company a brainwave. Shiok Meats aims to produce artificial shrimp, just as other firms are seeking to create artificial beef without cows. The process involves propagating shrimp cells in a nutrient-rich solution. Because prawn meat has a simpler structure than beef, it should be easier to replicate in this way. Moreover, shrimp is eaten in lots of forms and textures: whole, minced, as a paste, and so on. The company has already tested its shrimp mince in Chinese dumplings. Eventually it plans to grow curved "whole" shrimp – without the head and shell, that is. The hitch is that producing shrimp in this way currently costs $5,000 a kilogram. Shiok Meats thinks it can bring the price down dramatically as it refines and scales up its process. And even ordinary shrimp, whether farmed or fished, come at a higher environmental price than most people realise.

The-winter-that-wasn't of 2019–20

The most commonly cited risks of climate change are natural disasters: fiercer wildfires and hurricanes, bigger floods and longer droughts. But one of the most striking recent effects of global warming has been unusually mild weather in many parts of the world.

The northern-hemisphere winter that ended on March 20th 2020 was the second-warmest since records began, and the warmest ever on land. The anomaly was biggest in Europe and Asia, where average temperatures from December to February were 3.2°C (5.8°F) and 3.1°C above the average from 1951–80, and 0.8°C and 0.7°C above those continents' previous record highs. After a normal autumn, temperatures stayed close to their November levels for months. In Boston, where daily lows in January tend to hover around -6°C, the average minimum this January was 0°C; for Tokyo the figures were 0°C and 5°C. By local standards, the balmiest winter of all was in Russia. Moscow's average daily low in January was -2°C, far from the customary -13°C.

The winter-that-wasn't of 2019–20 is not yet a new normal. The main factor determining the severity of northern winters is the "Arctic oscillation": the relative pressure of Arctic and subtropical air. When pressure is higher in the Arctic, cold air from the North Pole pushes south, bringing harsh, dry winters to many places. When pressure is higher towards the subtropics, warm air pushes northwards, hemming in cold air around the pole. These two patterns flip back and forth irregularly. For reasons that are not yet clear, pressure in the subtropics in 2019–20 was much stronger than in the Arctic. And researchers have not yet determined how rising temperatures affect the Arctic oscillation. Until a few years ago, climate models tended to show pressure in the Arctic strengthening, reducing the amount of warming during winter at temperate northern latitudes. The latest models find the reverse.

The northern-hemisphere winter of 2019–20 was the warmest ever on land

---

Northern-hemisphere land temperature in winter, change from 1951 to 1980 average, °C

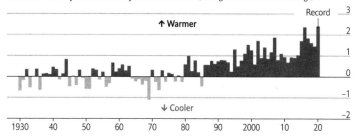

Average daily low temperature by month
Selected cities, °C

━ 2019–20*   ━ 1951–80 average

▨ 95% confidence interval

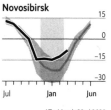

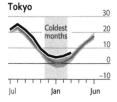
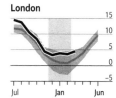
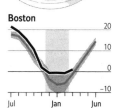

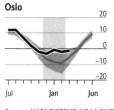
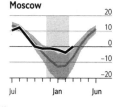

Sources: NASA GISTEMP; NOAA GHCND

*To March 23rd 2020

How do you define a heatwave?

In the summer of 2019 Europe sweltered in unusual temperatures. Germany, Poland and the Czech Republic saw record-breaking temperatures for June. France recorded its highest temperature – 45.1C (113.2F) – of all time. "Heatwave!", scream myriad headlines. But what exactly is a heatwave? According to the 1963 hit song "Heat Wave" by Martha and the Vandellas, a heatwave involves an inability to stop crying, the feeling of being possessed by the devil, high blood pressure and a "burning in my heart". That definition is a model of precision compared with the one provided by the World Meteorological Organisation (WMO), the UN agency that calls itself "the authoritative voice on the state and behaviour of the world's atmosphere". A heatwave, it says, is a "marked warming of the air, or the invasion of very warm air, over a large area; it usually lasts from a few days to a few weeks". To residents of cooler climes, that sounds quite pleasant, and utterly fails to capture the lethal menace of an extended spell of extreme temperatures. Is there not something more precise?

Governments have been late to the game when it comes to establishing exact criteria for heatwaves and public heat-warning systems. They have been more active since 2003, when stories about elderly people in France dying while their families were on holiday fed public outrage. And governments have also responded to the increased frequency of periods of extreme heat in recent years. Yet a survey by the WMO in 2015 found that around one-third of countries still lacked criteria for defining and reacting to heatwaves. Worryingly, there is still no commonly accepted definition for the point at which the public should be alerted.

Some differences make sense because heatwave warnings depend in part on what residents are used to. The temperatures that kept Parisians sweating on the Metro would barely warrant a mention in Furnace Creek, California, which has recorded the world's highest temperature (56.7°C, or 134°F, in 1913). So it makes sense to tailor warnings to local conditions. For example,

Environment Canada, a government department, warns residents of Prince Edward Island when the temperature is likely to reach 27°C, but sets a threshold for such warnings of 35°C for the arid interior of south-eastern British Columbia, where residents are used to higher temperatures.

Yet maximum temperature is only one of several variables that can add up to a killer heatwave. Others include humidity, air pollution, wind conditions, the minimum night-time temperature and how long the hot spell lasts. National definitions vary widely, depending on which of these variables are included, how they are measured, and even on the timing of warnings. An alert in England means the heatwave is expected within three days. In Belgium, it means the hot weather has already arrived.

The WMO is encouraging climate and health scientists to develop a measure that could be used more widely in forecasts and warnings. Many are in development, including a universal thermal climate index, which combines air temperature with measures of its effect on the human body. But for now, the answer to the question "what is a heatwave?" depends on where you are.

Speaking my language: words and wisdom

Why some languages are spoken faster than others

If this text was written in Japanese, it would be longer. A Thai translation, meanwhile, would be shorter. And yet those reading it aloud, in either language or in its original English, would finish at roughly the same time. This peculiar phenomenon is the subject of research which finds that languages face a trade-off between complexity and speed. Those packed with information are spoken slower, while simpler ones are spoken faster. As a result, most languages are equally efficient at conveying information.

In a study published in September 2019 in *Science Advances*,

Say no more

Syllable rate and information rate in selected languages

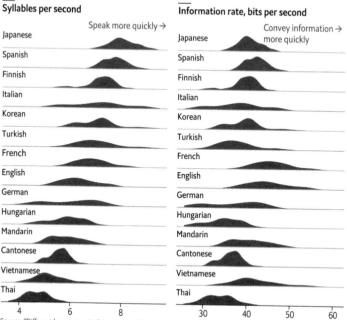

Syllables per second

Speak more quickly →

Japanese
Spanish
Finnish
Italian
Korean
Turkish
French
English
German
Hungarian
Mandarin
Cantonese
Vietnamese
Thai

4   6   8

Information rate, bits per second

Convey information → more quickly

Japanese
Spanish
Finnish
Italian
Korean
Turkish
French
English
German
Hungarian
Mandarin
Cantonese
Vietnamese
Thai

30   40   50   60

Source: "Different languages, similar encoding efficiency: comparable information rates across the human communicative niche", C. Coupé *et al.*, *Science Advances*, 2019

Christophe Coupé, Yoon Mi Oh, Dan Dediu and François Pellegrino started by quantifying the information density of 17 Eurasian languages, as measured by the ease with which each syllable could be guessed based on the preceding one. Next, they recorded the rate at which 170 native speakers read 15 texts out loud. Finally, armed with data about the information contained in a piece of text and the speed at which it can be spoken, the authors derived the rate at which information was being communicated.

The results suggest that there is an optimal range of speeds within which the brain can process information most efficiently. Speakers of simple languages pick up the pace to keep conversations brief. Speakers of complex languages exert more effort planning sentences and articulating syllables, causing discussions to drag on. Yet in both cases, information is conveyed at about the same pace. "It is like bird wings," says Dr Coupé, one of the authors. "You may have big ones that need few beats per second or you have to really flap the little ones. But the result is pretty much the same in terms of flying."

Where are the world's best English-speakers?

English is the most widely spoken language in the world. And of the roughly 1.5bn speakers globally, the vast majority speak it as a second language. So where are the world's best non-native English speakers? According to a report by EF Education First (EF), an international education company, Northern Europeans are the most fluent (the Netherlands tops the rankings, followed by Sweden, Norway and Denmark). Middle Easterners are the least proficient (Iraq, Kuwait, Oman and Saudi Arabia all rank near the bottom).

These results are not comprehensive, however. Nor are they representative. EF's index is based on the results of a free online test taken by 2.3m volunteers in 100 countries. Only people with an internet connection and time and willingness to take a test were included in the sample, which means the results are biased towards richer countries interested in English. As a result, many African countries do not have enough test-takers – at least 400 – to be included in the index. Such biases aside, the EF's index produces results that are interesting, if not entirely scientific. Nearly six in ten of 2019's test-takers were female. Women have always fared better than men, but in 2019 men closed the gap somewhat. Some countries saw their proficiency scores decline. This is probably not because their English got worse; more likely, a big increase in the number of test-takers brought in more people with weak English.

In Europe, the powerhouse economies fared surprisingly badly: only Germany made the top tier of "very high proficiency" countries. France was next, while Spain and Italy are persistent laggards. A study by a Spanish research institute confirmed the bad news: 60% of adults say they speak no English at all. The fact that Spanish is a global language in its own right (the language boasts 400m native speakers) is probably the culprit. If you speak Danish, you need another language to take part in global culture; speaking French or Spanish (or Arabic) gives you hundreds of millions of people to talk to without English.

Now you're speaking my language

English proficiency, 2018

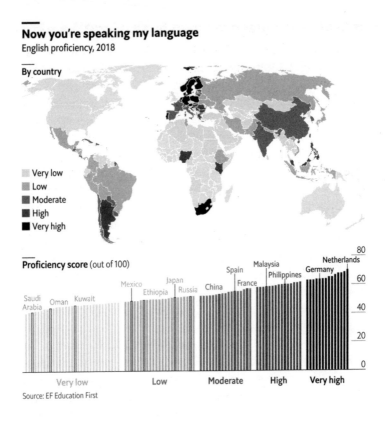

By country

Very low
Low
Moderate
High
Very high

Proficiency score (out of 100)

Source: EF Education First

Asia was the region of greatest diversity. Only Singapore made the top tier, but the Philippines, Malaysia, Hong Kong and India were not far behind. China was further back but still in the second tier, a few slots ahead of Japan. Languishing in the bottom slots were a clutch of South-East and Central Asian countries like Cambodia and Kyrgyzstan. This highlights another factor: EF repeatedly finds that English skills are highly correlated with connections and openness to the rest of the world.

Is Scots a language, or merely a dialect?

A majority of Scots rejected Brexit in the referendum of 2016, whereas a majority in the United Kingdom overall supported it. Scotland has now left the European Union against its will – prompting renewed calls for Scotland, in turn, to leave the UK. Naturally, the case for independence plays up characteristics that differentiate Scotland from England. Among them is language, which diverges from the talk south of the border in two main ways. One is Gaelic, a Celtic language impenetrable to outsiders (it is closely related to Irish and Manx but only distantly to English), which is spoken only by around 50,000 people, or about 1% of Scotland's population. The bigger difference is Scots – though quite how different it is remains a matter of debate.

As soon as you cross over from England, syntax and pronunciation change sharply. While the dialects of northern England have much in common with each other, the break at the border is stark. Because of that, some observers think Scots is not a dialect of English but a distinct (if related) language. The pro-independence Scottish National Party affirms as much in its manifesto. Pronunciation is not enough to make Scots a language, however, or the Geordie English spoken in the north-east of England would be one, too. But Scots also has its own vocabulary, which goes beyond the well-known "aye, bonnie lass" of films and television. Scots descends from Northumbrian, one of the dialects of Old English; standard southern English descends from a dialect based farther south. Scots retained Old English words that southern English lost, such as *bannock*. It was more influenced by Norse, in words such as *gate* (street) and *kirk* (church). It also has words from Gaelic, not just *loch* and *whisky* but *quaich* (a kind of bowl) and *sonse* (good luck). It also has its own Norman French borrowings, not shared with English, such as *douce* (sedate, sober).

Still, vocabulary does not make a language either. More fundamental still is grammar – and here, Scots stands out again. Its speakers say "I'm going to my bed" whereas the English say simply "to bed". "Dinnae" is a Scots version of "don't". "Div" commonly replaces the auxiliary verb "do". There are past-tense forms such as *jamp* (jumped), and irregular plurals like *een* (eyes) and *kye* (cows).

The Scots Syntax Atlas, free online, also shows how Scots varies internally. If you find a long-missing item, you might say "there it is" in English. But while, in other contexts, "it is" contracts to "it's", you can't say "there it's!" – save in a belt of Scotland running roughly from Kilmarnock to Edinburgh. People in that belt are unlikely to say "so apparently himself is joining us for dinner," while northern, highland and some island Scots do.

There is no consensus among professional linguists as to whether, in aggregate, these features make Scots a language, or merely a dialect. Geoffrey Pullum, an Englishman at the University of Edinburgh, leans towards language status. Despite his expertise (and living in Scotland), he "simply cannot understand two Scots-speaking workers when they are chatting with each other". He emphasises those grammatical differences, as well as the long literary history of Scots. But David Adger, a Scot at Queen Mary University of London (and, like Mr Pullum, a specialist in syntax), is unconvinced. He studies Scots as one among many varieties of English. After all, people who speak it can vary their delivery from broad Scots to Scottish-accented standard English on a smooth continuum, depending on the circumstances.

This makes Scots and English different from, say, Danish and Norwegian. Speakers of those related tongues understand each other with few problems. But they are not in the habit of making transitions between the two – they speak one or the other. Politics is integral to the divide: Norwegian was consciously developed away from Danish as part of a push for independence. As an old saying goes, "a language is a dialect with an army and a navy". Recognition for Scots as a language may, ultimately, be clinched not by grammatical arguments but by political ones. Proclaiming it to be a language to support Scottish independence may have little impact. But if Scotland gains independence, outsiders might take Scots seriously as a separate language, too.

How new is the singular "they" pronoun?

Grammar has rarely produced as much public acrimony as in the battle over pronouns being waged around the world. In one skirmish in 2015, the University of Tennessee offered guidance on referring to non-binary students on its website, only for political blowback to lead to a legislative ban on spending public money to support non-traditional pronouns. Jordan Peterson, a controversial Canadian academic, has refused to use invented pronouns or "they" in relation to people who identify as neither male nor female. Many fulminating commentators spy political correctness running amok yet again. Into the breach comes a useful corrective in the form of Dennis Baron's book, *What's Your Pronoun?* Mr Baron is a linguist at the University of Illinois, and a long-time scholar of a curious gap in the English language. For centuries, he explains, people have wrestled with the fact that there is no uncontroversial pronoun to refer to a subject of unknown, indeterminate or mixed gender.

Singular *they*, in sentences such as "Everyone loves their mother", has been derided as incorrect for a long time. Mr Baron tracks the first such ruling to a 16th-century Latin grammar, which declared that masculine, where necessary, encompasses the feminine. In the 18th and 19th centuries, this view made its way into English grammars: when referring to a generic person, you should say "Everyone loves his mother." But there were wide holes in this argument. Proponents of the rule treated it as a simple matter of grammatical agreement: *everyone* is grammatically singular, so requires a singular pronoun. *They* is plural and won't do. To real sticklers for agreement, however, pronouns must tally in both number and gender. Generic *they* is wrong by number, but generic *he* is wrong by gender.

Nonetheless, "*he* includes *she*" was in textbooks, and so, for a time, proto-feminists tried to take advantage where they could. Laws saying that each person should pay "his" taxes required women to pay, too. So, 19th-century suffragists reasoned, the statute books referring to a generic voter as "he" gave women the right to vote. Seemingly hoist on the chauvinist petard, defenders of male-only suffrage tactically retreated: *he* included *she* unless it would produce an "absurd" reading – such as offering women the vote. (Since it was often held that husbands voted in their wives' interests, Susan B. Anthony, a 19th-century American suffragist, suggested that if a woman commits murder her husband should be hanged in her stead.)

Given the problems with *he*, lots of people have invented new, gender-free pronouns. The first one Mr Baron could find (of more than 250 in total) dates to 1841: *E*. Other suggestions continue in a steady stream until today. Every once in a while, one found a tiny purchase. In 1884 three dictionaries included *thon*, shortened from *that one*, but it failed to catch on. The *Sacramento Bee*, a newspaper, said in 1920 that it would use *hir* in place of "he or she", and did so sporadically until the 1940s, but it too faded away. The "missing word", Mr Baron says, is "they". People have been using it as a generic singular in writing since at least 1375, and have doubtless been saying it even longer. It has appeared as such in the King James Bible, the works of Shakespeare and the novels of Jane Austen. Recently, growing numbers of style guides, including those of *The Economist* and the Associated Press as well as the *Chicago Manual of Style*, have concluded that it is often the most pragmatic of a set of imperfect solutions.

But all that comes as a different singular *they* has come to the fore: to refer to a known individual who identifies as non-binary, as growing numbers do, in sentences such as "Alex forgot their keys." This is the increasingly widespread singular *they* that was recognised in January 2020 by the American Dialect Society as its Word of the Decade. The two usages are quite different. The one in "Everyone has their own opinion" is actually quite conservative, given its age, its literary pedigree and the fact that most people already say it in casual speech. *They* in "Alex forgot their keys" is, by contrast, innovative and jarring to many; for the uninitiated, it takes practice to use it consistently. And though both feminists and transgender activists have embraced the singular *they*, they have done so for different reasons, and other issues still divide them. A rare moment of liberation through grammar risks being caught up in wider, rancorous culture wars.

Why foreign languages remain a coveted skill in Britain

Londoners hoping to work for Gucci, an Italian fashion retailer, may be surprised by the skills required. As well as knowledge of luxury products, including accessories and leather goods, and industry trends, candidates to be a "brand ambassador" at the outlet in Harrods need something extra. Because the posh department store's customers include rich visitors from the Gulf, you must also be able to speak Arabic.

Foreign languages are a coveted skill in Britain, according to an analysis of data from Indeed, a recruitment website. Of the millions of jobs in Britain listed there, around one in 200 requires foreign languages. German and French, the most desirable languages, feature in about 115 out of every 100,000 postings, more than twice as often as Chinese, Italian or Spanish. Twenty-nine in 100,000 listings require Dutch; 20 call for Japanese, Polish or Russian. Despite the rise of translation software, people prefer to be served by fellow humans who can speak their mother tongue.

Different languages crop up more often in different trades. German is favoured in both sales and customer service, French in sales and education. A lot of mums and dads in London want their nannies to speak Russian. Rich folk seeking "lifestyle managers" are likely to want Arabic. Beauty consultants fluent in Mandarin are also in demand. According to Pawel Adrjan, an economist at Indeed, the supply of foreign-language speakers is less seasonal than that for most workers, because many do not take time off for Christmas.

Although demand for language skills remains robust, supply is being choked. The share of children in British secondary schools who learn a foreign language is at its lowest level in almost 20 years. Employers are turning to foreign native speakers to meet demand for foreign-language teachers, interpreters, translators and bilingual customer-service representatives. But Brexit has restricted this source of supply. Searches on Indeed's website for jobs in Britain requiring European languages other than English

Slip of the tongues

Foreign language searches on Indeed.co.uk, per 100,000 total searches

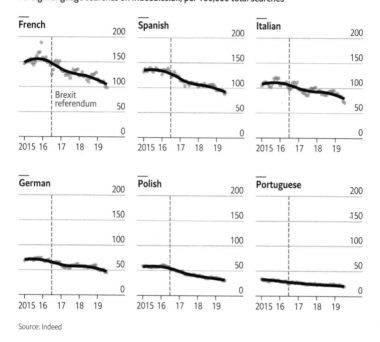

Source: Indeed

have been on the decline. Since the 2016 referendum, those for positions demanding Polish have fallen by almost half.

How the internet is helping explain how language works

What is technology doing to language? Many assume the answer is simple: ruining it. Kids can no longer write except in text-speak. Grammar is going to the dogs. The ability to compose thoughts longer than a tweet is waning. Language experts tend to resist that gloom, noting that there is little proof that speech is really degenerating: kids may say "lol" out loud sometimes, but this is a marginal phenomenon. Nor is formal writing falling apart. Sentences like "OMG WTF William teh Conqueror pwned Harold at Hastings in 1066!" tend to be written by middle-aged columnists trying to imitate children's supposed habits. A study by Cambridge Assessment, a British exam-setter, found almost no evidence for text-speak in students' writing. Fortunately, the story of language and the internet has attracted more serious analysts, too. Gretchen McCulloch, a prolific language blogger and journalist – and herself of the generation that grew up with the internet – has joined them with her book, *Because Internet: Understanding the New Rules of Language*. Rather than obsessing about what the internet is doing to language, it largely focuses on what can be learned about language from the internet.

For example, why do languages change? A thousand years ago, early versions of English and Icelandic were closely related, possibly even mutually intelligible. English has since evolved hugely, and Icelandic, far less. Linguists have studied the relative effects of strong ties (friends, family) and weaker acquaintanceships in such patterns, hypothesising that small communities would host more stable languages. A computer simulation proved that a mix of strong and weak ties – close-knit groups existing in a larger sea – allowed language-change "leaders" to disseminate updates to the wider population. Twitter combines strong and weak ties – and sure enough, drives more language change than Facebook, which is more dominated by strong ties. That, in turn, helps explain the conservatism of Icelandic (more like Facebook) and the mutability of English (more like Twitter).

Emoji, odd as they may look, also reflect something universal. They are not a language (try telling a complex story in emoji to someone who doesn't know it already). They are, Ms McCulloch argues, the digital equivalent of gestures. Those come in two types. "Emblems", like a thumbs-up or a wink, have a fixed meaning and form. But "co-speech" gestures – wincing, gesticulating, pointing – are spontaneous and more variable. And emoji come in these same flavours. People randomly combine many co-speech-style emoji, but are more restrained in mixing emblems. Just as it would make no sense to give someone the finger while shaking your head to negate it, emblematic emoji often stand alone rather than in expressive chains.

Other online "innovations" are not really new, either. Philosophers have previously tried to invent a marker for irony – a backwards question-mark or an upside-down exclamation point, for example – before online types succeeded with the sarcastic ~tilde~. The first use of OMG long preceded computers. Those who worry about teens speaking "hashtag" aloud ("Good for you – hashtag sarcasm!") might consider the last time they punctuated an utterance by saying "full stop" or "period".

So the internet age has given rise to a new medium rather than a new language. For millennia, speech was all there was. For most of "recorded" history, nearly everyone was illiterate. Then, in the age of the printing press and mass literacy, writing acquired a kind of primacy, seen as prestigious, a standard to be learned and imitated (often even in speech). Future historians may regard that epoch of reverence as unusual. Mass reading has now been joined by mass writing: frequent, error-filled and evanescent – like speech. Little surprise that internet users have created tools to give their writing the gesture, playfulness and even meaninglessness of chitchat. Mistaking it for the downfall of "real" writing is a category error. Anything that helps people enjoy each other's company can only be a good thing.

Why so many Australians speak Arabic

Maps of languages often look deceptively simple: language X is spoken here, language Y there. But people have a habit of moving around, and maps are not good at showing complicated mixtures of languages. So NeoMam Studios, a British design firm, has broken out the first-, second- and, most interestingly, third-most-spoken languages in almost every country in the world. The results are surprising. Although many people could probably guess that the second-most spoken languages in Canada and America are French and Spanish, respectively, those ranked third are less easy to guess: Punjabi in Canada and Chinese (including both Mandarin and Cantonese) in America. Similarly, reflecting a history of immigration from North Africa and the Middle East, Arabic is the third-most-spoken language in Australia, spoken by 1.4% of speakers in 2017, up from 0.1% in 2011.

In some countries the third-ranked language is an indigenous one. In populous places, this can result in an otherwise obscure tongue outperforming better-known counterparts. Marathi, spoken in the Indian state of Maharashtra, has more than 80m native speakers, putting it on par globally with German. Wu, a variety of Chinese spoken in Shanghai and neighbouring Zhejiang and Jiangsu provinces, is listed as China's third-biggest language. It too has about 80m native speakers.

The case of different forms of Chinese shows just one way in which tabulating such things can quickly get messy. How non-native speakers of a language are treated is another problem: English has been taught to hundreds of millions of Chinese and Indians, but the CIA's *The World Factbook*, from which NeoMam gets much of its data, does not list English among the top three languages in either country. By one estimate, around 10% of Indians speak English, which would make it the country's second-biggest language.

NeoMam's sources, the CIA's *The World Factbook* and *Ethnologue*, a standard reference work on the world's languages, also treat immigrant languages inconsistently. Turkish, which is almost

Un, deux, trois... parlez!
Third-most-spoken language, 2019

Language family

■ Sino-Tibetan   ■ Indo-European   ■ Afro-Asiatic   ■ Niger-Congo   Other*   No data

Sources: NeoMam Studios; CIA *World Factbook*; *Ethnologue*   *Including Creole languages

certainly Germany's second-most-spoken native language, is absent from NeoMam's list of the country's top three languages. Chuck Fennig, managing editor of *Ethnologue*, explains that the database treats Turkish as an immigrant language in Germany, not a native one. The moral of the story is that, when attempting to add detail to the world's language map, it is easy to get tongue-tied.

How to talk to aliens

Imagine dining in a European capital where you do not know the local language. The waiter speaks little English, but by hook or by crook you manage to order something on the menu that you recognise, eat and pay for. Now picture instead that, after a hike goes wrong, you emerge, starving, in an Amazonian village. The people there have no idea what to make of you. You mime chewing sounds, which they mistake for your primitive tongue. When you raise your hands to signify surrender, they think you are launching an attack.

Communicating without a shared context is hard. For example, radioactive sites must be left undisturbed for tens of thousands of years; yet, given that the English of just 1,000 years ago is now unintelligible to most of its modern speakers, agencies have struggled to create warnings to accompany nuclear waste. Committees responsible for doing so have come up with everything from towering concrete spikes, to Edvard Munch's *The Scream*, to plants genetically modified to turn an alarming blue. None is guaranteed to be future-proof. Some of the same people who worked on these waste-site messages have also been part of an even bigger challenge: communicating with extraterrestrial life.

Nothing is known about how extraterrestrials might take in information. A pair of plaques sent in the early 1970s with *Pioneer 10* and *Pioneer 11*, two spacecraft, show nude human beings and a rough map to find Earth – rudimentary stuff, but even that assumes aliens can see. Since such craft have no more than an infinitesimal chance of being found, radio broadcasts from Earth, travelling at the speed of light, are more likely to make contact. But just as a terrestrial radio must be tuned to the right frequency, so must the interstellar kind. How would aliens happen upon the correct one? The *Pioneer* plaque gives a hint in the form of a basic diagram of a hydrogen atom, the magnetic polarity of which flips at regular intervals, with a frequency of 1,420MHz. Since hydrogen is the most abundant element in the universe, the hope is that this sketch might act as a sort of telephone number. Assuming that human messages actually reach their target, what would earthlings and aliens talk about? The obvious subject to focus on is mathematics; its basic concepts are often assumed to be universal. Any intelligent species might have an interest in natural numbers (1, 2, 3 and so on) as well as things such as *pi*. But moving beyond that to wider conversation would be far harder. Scientists have worked on "self-interpreting" languages – written in a way that aims to teach the reader the language as they go – which might make the next steps possible.

Is there any reason to think alien communication systems would share the two key design features of human language, words and grammar? A word like "book" is a symbol for all objects that exhibit bookish qualities; would aliens also employ symbols, rather than having separate names for every object in their world? Perhaps. Whatever type of society they inhabit, alien life-forms would have limited time and energy, as people do. It is efficient to use symbols. Similarly, human grammar allows a vast number of sentences to be made from a finite number of rules. Any resource-constrained Moon-people might develop such grammar, too.

Even if all such hurdles were overcome, however, distance would still be a problem. Human children learn their first language by listening, trying it out and getting instant feedback. This give-and-take allows them to use fluent sentences by the age of four. In 2015 the first known exoplanet at a "Goldilocks" distance from its star (not too near and not too far), and with water, was discovered 110 light-years away. A message sent today would arrive in 110 years' time; its reply, 110 years after that. The kinds of exchanges depicted in sci-fi films would take lifetimes. The awesome challenges of communicating across the galaxy mean that some think it not worth the effort. But pondering these obstacles raises another thought, not about aliens but what humanity has in common. Linguists argue about whether languages share universal features or are unique products of local cultures. But whatever the answer, the world's 7,000-odd tongues are vastly closer to one another than anything to be found out there.

That's entertainment: art, sport and culture

Why music charts ain't what they used to be

It sold more than 45m copies, provided bedroom poster art to countless youngsters and propelled Pink Floyd, then a relatively obscure English rock band, to international stardom. *The Dark Side of the Moon* has earned countless accolades since its release in 1973. Among its most extraordinary achievements is the time it spent on America's Billboard 200 album chart: 943 weeks, the equivalent of 18 years. Such feats are becoming ever less common, according to a paper by Lukas Schneider and Claudius Gros of the Goethe University in Frankfurt. Their study, which analyses music charts in America, Britain, Germany and the Netherlands going back to 1979, finds that today's pop stars have to jostle with more of their fellow artists to gain the top spot. Whereas three decades ago any given year might produce about a dozen number-one albums, these days there are around 40. Popular music has become more varied as a result.

As competition has increased, artists' journeys up the rankings have accelerated. For much of the past five decades, albums took more than a month to climb to the top (*Dark Side* entered the Billboard charts at number 95). These days, if an album does not immediately reach number one, it is unlikely ever to do so. Artists are falling out of the rankings more quickly, too. In the 1970s, an album's final position in the 200-album chart (before dropping out altogether) was 100 on average. Today it is typically 75. A successful album spends less than half as long in the charts as it did 25 years ago. The authors offer several explanations for their findings. The internet and the growth of smartphones have given music-lovers immediate access to new music, allowing them to buy or download albums with a single click. Streaming services, meanwhile, have made the listening experience more personal. Popular taste, the authors argue, has consequently become both more fragmented and more volatile.

One piece of evidence for this is the proliferation of new charts. There are so many charts that a company called Chartmetric even offers to follow them for music-industry professionals who cannot keep up. The more charts there are, the less meaning they hold, and the harder it is to use them for their specific purpose: measuring one artist's success relative to another. If someone is top of YouTube's video chart, but number 20 in Spotify's weekly songs chart, are they more or less popular than someone who is number eight in both? What if someone completely different is top of Britain's Official Chart (based on a combination of sales, streams and downloads)?

The issue may seem to be a trifling one, but it does matter. The proliferation of charts makes it harder to discern who is and who is not a big cheese. It is clear who the stars of the movie business are because box-office receipts provide an easy metric by which to measure their wattage. Whether you are a teenager or a pensioner, you have a rough idea of who the biggest film stars are at any given moment, and there is cultural common ground. That is no longer the case with pop. Thirty years ago, an average parent and an average teenager would probably both have known the biggest hitmakers of the year. There was one chart, and because there was only one, it mattered. Now, even a music-savvy parent is likely to have no idea who is number one (and nor, very possibly, might their child). Music has become subject to cultural and generational silos. The job of critics and historians, in turn, has become trickier.

When was greatness thrust upon William Shakespeare?

"He was not of an age, but for all time," wrote Ben Jonson, a peer of William Shakespeare, in the preface to the *First Folio* – a collection of the bard's works published in 1623, seven years after he died. Today, those words seem prophetic. In Jonson's time, they were mostly just polite. Shakespeare was popular in his day; his company drew large crowds at the Globe Theatre in London, and sometimes performed at court. But other authors of his era were more acclaimed. Francis Beaumont was buried in Poets' Corner at Westminster Abbey, near Geoffrey Chaucer. Jonson received a royal pension for writing. When Shakespeare died, few would have guessed that all the world would become his stage.

A newly digitised version of *The London Stage*, a record of performances from 1660 to 1800, tracks Shakespeare's ascent to unquestioned supremacy. Mattie Burkert, the project's leader, says the data are patchy between 1660, when theatres reopened after a Puritan ban, and 1700, when daily newspapers began. Moreover, attributing shows to authors is tricky, because most were advertised without naming the playwright. Nonetheless, of 2,300 events recorded in this period, just 122 (5%) included material that might have been by Shakespeare. The data give more credits to two newer writers, John Fletcher (with 191) and John Dryden (137). Courtiers preferred libertine heroes and neo-classical styles. Shakespeare's untutored mingling of fools and kings seemed odd, so dramatists often rewrote his texts.

Shakespeare's star began to rise a century after his death. Fiona Ritchie, a scholar who specialises in his 18th-century reputation, notes a few causes. Some adaptations of his work, such as a version of *King Lear* with a happy ending, became popular. In the 1730s the Shakespeare Ladies' Club, a group of aristocratic women, petitioned theatre-owners to stage his plays rather than foreign operas. Comedies such as *Twelfth Night* and *As You Like It*, now featuring female actresses, came back into fashion. Even as the appetite for

Shakespeare is as pre-eminent in London today as he was 200 years ago, but the city's favourite plays have changed

—
Past and present popularity of plays
Share of Shakespearean performances*, %

● Comedies ● Histories ● Tragedies

← More popular then   More popular now →

Macbeth
Richard III
Romeo & Juliet

Othello

8%

The Tempest
The Merchant of Venice
The Merry Wives of Windsor

6

Henry VIII

The Taming of the Shrew
Cymbeline
Julius Caesar

Measure for Measure

Timon of Athens

King John

4

2

0

A Midsummer Night's Dream

Hamlet

Twelfth Night

As You Like It

Much Ado About Nothing

King Lear

Richard II
The Winter's Tale
Henry IV, Part 1
The Comedy of Errors
Antony and Cleopatra
Henry V
Henry IV, Part 2
All's Well That Ends Well
Love's Labour's Lost
Pericles
Coriolanus
Henry VI, Part 1
Titus Andronicus
Henry VI, Parts 2 and 3
Two Gentlemen of Verona
Troilus and Cressida
Two Noble Kinsmen

1660–1800   2000–19   1660–1800   2000–19

Sources: London Stage Database; UK Theatre Web   *Includes adaptations by other authors

comedies grew, eminent actors – above all David Garrick – used sturdier roles, such as Richard III and Macbeth, to boost their careers. In 1769 Garrick organised a jubilee of Shakespeare's birth, to celebrate "the god of our idolatry". Shakespeare has had god-like status ever since. Harold Bloom, a critic, called his plays "the outward limit of human achievement".

By 1800, 9% of shows in London used his material – down from a peak of 17%, but much more than his rivals. Today, Londoners still lend him their ears. Using listings from UK Theatre Web, an online archive, we estimate that the city's big theatres have put on 360,000 performances since 2000 (including musicals and operas, to mimic the older data). Of those, Shakespeare accounts for some 19,000, or 5%. Although this share is similar to that in the 17th century, it is far more impressive, because Shakespeare must now compete with thousands of writers who had not been born in 1700. *A Midsummer Night's Dream*, once seen as insipid, is now the most performed play. But the split among comedies, tragedies and histories remains similar to that in 1740–1800. It was the thespians of that age who prepared him for all time.

How "speedcubers" are getting faster

It was hailed as the world's first "sub-4". On November 24th 2018, Yusheng Du, a Chinese Rubik's Cube enthusiast, solved a standard 3x3x3 cube in an astonishing 3.47 seconds. The feat, now an official Guinness World Record, smashed the previous record by 0.75 seconds. Speedcubing is a relatively new phenomenon. Erno Rubik, a Hungarian scientist, patented the original cube in 1974 (his first attempt at cracking it took several weeks). Made up of nine coloured squares on each of its six faces, the cube rotates around a central axis. By twisting the sides, the cube's colours can be scrambled and unscrambled. When solved, each side of the cube is a solid colour.

After a global craze in the 1980s, the puzzle's popularity gradually faded; it was propelled back from oblivion by the internet. Mass-circulated instructions, YouTube tutorials and online clubs and forums all helped to re-popularise the cube. A world championship was reintroduced in 2003, after a 19-year hiatus. Over the years, the record for solving the cube has been gradually whittled down to near-superhuman speeds. Beyond the classic competition, cubers also race to solve the puzzle one-handed, with their feet, while blindfolded and even underwater.

Techniques for solving a Rubik's Cube include the Corners-First method, the Petrus method and the advanced Fridrich method (the one used by Mr Yusheng). Although the classic 3x3x3 cube has a mind-boggling number of possible configurations (more than 43 quintillion), solving it never requires more than 20 moves; most configurations require just 18. But for speedcubers, there are other factors to consider. The World Cube Association allows players to lubricate and sand their cubes' mechanisms to improve their times. But too much fiddling can be risky: damage or markings can result in disqualification. The arrival of magnetised cubes in 2016 has enabled more accurate twisting, helping to shave off valuable milliseconds.

For some, a puzzle that was initially designed to stimulate complex mathematical calculations has become a fiercely

One good turn deserves another
Rubik's Cube world record times*

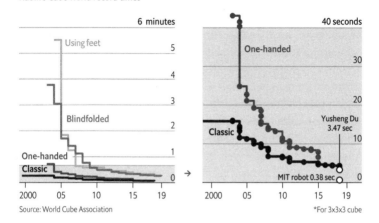

Source: World Cube Association

*For 3x3x3 cube

competitive test of muscle memory, rote learning and luck (Mr Yusheng's sub-4 benefited from a fortunate initial "scramble"). For others, speedcubing is more light-hearted. In 2018 a 13-year-old Chinese boy went viral after setting world records for solving three Rubik's Cubes simultaneously while juggling them (5 minutes 6.61 seconds) or by using both hands and feet (1 minute 36.39 seconds). Mr Yusheng, for his part, may have room for improvement. In 2016 a German-built robot solved a Cube in a blur lasting 0.637 seconds. In March 2018 a robot built by two American engineering students, Ben Katz and Jared Di Carlo, did better still. The machine, which was outfitted with PlayStation Eye cameras and could execute a move in 15 milliseconds, solved the Cube in just 0.38 seconds.

Why athletes sometimes vanish

Halfway through the weightlifting competition at the Commonwealth games in Australia in April 2018, the Rwandan coach, Jean Paul Nsengiyumva, excused himself to go to the bathroom. He never came back. Mr Nsengiyumva was one of 250-odd competitors and support staff who disappeared over the course of the games. Cameroon lost a third of its delegation in three night-time absc1sions. Peter Dutton, the minister in charge of Australia's crackdown against asylum-seekers, said that he would find those remaining in the country illegally and "lock them in a local watch-house". But organisers did not seem surprised. "It happens at every games," shrugged Peter Beattie, who chaired the organising committee.

Athletes have long used competitions as an opportunity to escape war, poverty or repressive dictatorships, either by lodging claims for asylum or by disappearing altogether. Competitors and coaches have stayed behind at almost every Olympics since the second world war. Nearly half of Hungary's 100-strong delegation defected at the Melbourne Olympics of 1956, shortly after Soviet forces had quashed a revolution in their country. Some 145 athletes missed their outbound flights after the Sydney Olympics at the turn of this century too. And when Australia hosted the Commonwealth games in 2006, at least 40 participants stayed behind. Countries including Cuba and North Korea have been known to keep their athletes under surveillance to avoid losing entire teams.

The disappearances at the Commonwealth games in Australia were substantial even by the standards of this long tradition. Immigration officials told senators that roughly 190 of the absconding athletes had applied for asylum, with a handful more seeking other visas. That left 50-odd in the country illegally. Their numbers pale by comparison, however, to the thousands of asylum-seekers who arrive in Australia by other means each year. Few have made it in by sea since politicians resumed a bipartisan policy of putting "boat people" into detention centres on Pacific islands in 2013. But between 2015 and 2016 more than 9,500 individuals entered the country on valid visas – as tourists or business travellers, for example – and then stayed to lodge asylum claims. Much like the sports stars, some use religious gatherings or international conferences as opportunities to do so.

Mr Dutton, an immigration hardliner who once offered asylum to white farmers from South Africa, warned the disappearing athletes that they would not be able to "game the system". Yet with many hailing from poor or conflict-ridden African nations such as Sierra Leone and Cameroon, refugee agencies pointed out that they had every right to seek asylum. All 14 athletes who left Sierra Leone's Commonwealth team in 2006 were granted asylum in Australia. Some past defectors have even ended up competing for their adopted countries.

Why racing pigeons are so valuable

Meet Armando. He is five years old, looks alert – thanks to some striking red eyes – and has a neck coloured with vibrant green and pink streaks. He is also a champion. In 2018 he won the equivalent of national, European and Olympic gold medals. When put up for sale online, in March 2019, he attracted interest from all around the world, as well as his native Belgium. His new, Chinese owner paid €1.25m ($1.41m) for him, more than three times the previous online-auction record. This made Armando the world's most expensive racing pigeon. Why have elite birds become so costly?

Pigeon-racing has its roots in Belgium, where the first long-distance races were held in the 19th century and where colombophiles (pigeon fanciers) were common. The reputation of Belgian birds as the world's finest is a consequence of myriad generations of breeding and careful handling. But the biggest market for prize pigeons is China. Keeping pigeons and improving their homing instincts has long been popular, but racing the birds was banned during the Cultural Revolution because of its association with capitalism. The sport has boomed recently, especially at the top end. All the eye-popping purchases of elite birds, such as Bolt (€310,000 in 2013), Nadine (€400,000 in 2017) and New Bliksem (€376,000 in 2018), were made by Chinese bidders. Armando's price was driven up by two competing Chinese buyers. Indeed, pigeon racing in China is witnessing the same price inflation as many other asset classes, from fine wine to footballers. A supporting infrastructure has sprung up that encourages lavish spending on pedigree homers. The Pioneer International Club, based in Beijing, hosts a series of races known as the Iron Eagle, where pigeons fly distances of up to 500km for prize pots worth millions of dollars.

The luxury-goods market in China, which includes splurging on expensive hobbies such as prize pigeons, has been squeezed by the US-China trade war and the economic turmoil following the covid-19 outbreak. That said, the market for the priciest Belgian birds is highly concentrated, and is limited to a handful of fanciers whose prospects are crucial for the market. What is clear is that Armando's days of long-distance flying are over. Racing is dangerous, even for experienced birds, and expensive pigeons bought at auction are often not risked again. Armando's value lies in his genes: his buyer matched him with a pedigree hen, in the hope that his descendants would prove similarly adept. Indeed, seven of Armando's previous offspring were sold in the same auction as he was, raising over €150,000. Despite his hefty price tag, in short, the world's most expensive pigeon could eventually turn a profit for his new owner.

Why spoilers don't really spoil anything

In the first few decades of cinema, patrons would buy a ticket that granted general admission to the theatre. Several features would be playing on a loop, and you could choose whichever you fancied. You might enter halfway through the main movie, watch it until the end, see the cartoons and the newsreel and then start from the beginning to catch what you'd missed. It functioned rather like a big public television. Then, in 1960, a director decreed that no one would be permitted to enter screenings once his new film had begun: the integrity of the viewing experience was paramount. The film was *Psycho* and Alfred Hitchcock's edict – part artistic statement, part marketing ploy – placed new emphasis on plot twists in the final act. (He also asked critics not to discuss those key details.)

Today, writers and film-makers are obsessed with spoilers. J.K. Rowling has urged those watching *Harry Potter and the Cursed Child*, a stage play, to "keep the secrets". Anthony and Joseph Russo, the directors of Marvel films, have issued statements requesting that fans not ruin them for others. Audiences are zealous about the matter, too. Many viewers will go offline prior to episodes of a favourite television show, or mute certain words on social media to avoid seeing potentially spoiling posts. Writers must declare that their review contains spoilers, or face a backlash. One fan was assaulted outside a screening of *Avengers: Endgame* for "loudly revealing" the movie's outcome.

Narratives have always had twists and unforeseen turns. *Citizen Kane* (1941) reveals a crucial detail in the last minute; whodunnits keep audiences guessing until a last gasp-inducing denouement. But it was in films of the 1990s such as *The Crying Game*, *Seven*, *The Usual Suspects* and *Fight Club* that the twist ending came of age; M. Night Shyamalan, a writer and director, became something of a master of the form. The ascendancy of the twist coincided with the spread of the internet, and the spoiler hysteria began. With so much analysis of films and television online, new rules of debate were inaugurated whereby warnings must be given about spoilers, or readers must be allowed to opt in to them. Film-makers realised that fans were invested in the surprise and pandered to them. Joseph McGinty Nichol released false spoilers for *Terminator: Salvation*; other directors shoot multiple endings for their films.

Yet this attitude stifles proper discussion of stories by critics as much as viewers, and it inflicts damage on storytelling as a craft. By promoting one technique, the twist, and one effect, surprise, stories get bent out of shape. They try too hard to counter expectation and resist predictability. *The Lord of the Rings* is totally predictable from beginning to end, but the series does not suffer for it. William Shakespeare gave away the end of his tragedies by billing them as such and no one seemed to mind (*Romeo and Juliet* even told the audience the story in a prologue). *Columbo*, a classic crime serial, reveals who committed the murder at the beginning of each episode and succeeded in making the investigation thrilling to watch. Stories that promote surprise over character end up as mere soap opera, a series of sensational shocks. That corrodes credibility, while some reveals – it was all a dream! – do not so much blow minds as waste time. More significant than all of this, though, is the fact that surprise is overrated. A study carried out by Jonathan Leavitt and Nicholas Christenfeld of the University of California, San Diego, in 2011 found that knowing how the story ends doesn't hamper enjoyment – it increases it. Fittingly, the researchers announced their conclusion in the title of their paper: "Story spoilers don't spoil stories".

Why yacht rock came back into fashion

Put on a "yacht rock" playlist, and an image starts to form in your mind: one of ocean views from California's Highway 1, cold beers and blood-orange sunsets. The sound is smooth, with a soft bassline and minimal drums, and it combines elements of funk, jazz and R'n'B. The piano carries the melody, but often gives way to gentle guitar or saxophone solos. The lyrics might explore what it means to live a carefree life, but melancholic themes recur, too – particularly yearning or foolish love.

The subgenre, known at the time as soft rock or adult-oriented rock, was born in Los Angeles and San Francisco in the early 1970s. Many of those who had protested against war and preached free love in the decade before had grown up, settled down and bought homes and cars. Songwriters found a home for their gently catchy tunes on radio stations that were aimed at drivetime listeners. Seals and Crofts's appealing "Summer Breeze" (1972) was an early hit, soon followed by Steely Dan's "Reelin' in the Years". The Doobie Brothers dominated the airwaves with their more upbeat, finger-tapping rhythms in songs such as "It Keeps You Runnin'" (1976) and the Grammy award-winning "What a Fool Believes" (1979). Toto perfected the form in "Africa", which reached the number one spot on America's Billboard Hot 100 chart in 1983, and in "Rosanna".

But listeners soon tired of the music's earnestness. MTV had launched in 1981 and was keenly promoting New Wave music, which relied heavily on electronic sounds. Compared with Duran Duran's "Rio", Hall and Oates's "I Can't Go For That" lacked boldness and urgency. Other music fans had turned to the grittier and less aspirational tunes provided by alternative-rock bands such as R.E.M., and soft rock came to be dismissed as schmaltzy and uncool, consigned to wedding parties and dusty record collections.

Now it has come back into fashion again. An online series, released in 2005, dramatised the careers of American soft-rock stars and coined the term "yacht rock". An official playlist on Spotify has hundreds of thousands of followers. Toto's "Africa" enjoys enormous popularity: its video, first released in 1983, has been watched more than 550m times on YouTube. Google searches for "yacht rock" have steadily climbed since the early 2010s, with spikes in traffic in the summer months. *I Can Go for That: The Smooth World of Yacht Rock*, a two-part documentary, was broadcast on the BBC in June 2019. With this renewed attention has come some debate over what qualifies as yacht rock. The Spotify playlist features artists such as George Michael, Billy Joel and Fleetwood Mac alongside Journey, Foreigner and Kenny Loggins. The term "roughly corrals music that shares a DNA", says Katie Puckrik, the host of *I Can Go For That*. It is not "groundbreaking, manifesto-making music", she says, but "a mellow, easy, teflon-covered sound".

That DNA is evident in the work of modern hitmakers: listen to "Fragments of Time" by Daft Punk, "Fun, Fun, Fun" by Pharrell Williams (a self-confessed Steely Dan fan) and "White Sky" by Vampire Weekend and you will find the same light melodies. *Late Night Feelings*, Mark Ronson's most recent album, brings modern production techniques to bear on the same retro sound. Thundercat took his tribute to the era even further, featuring vocals from Michael McDonald and Kenny Loggins on his song "Show You The Way". People may be tuning in to yacht rock now for the same reason they did in the 1970s and early '80s. Back then the music provided a blissful escape from the news of the Watergate scandal, the bloody end of the Vietnam war, the energy crisis and economic stagnation. It lifted you out of your car or your office, and transported you to sunny California. The presidential scandals may be different, and new economic and environmental anxieties have arisen, but the satisfaction provided by a feel-good tune remains the same.

What explains the enduring popularity of *Friends*?

"Look around, you guys," says Chandler Bing to his newly adopted twins, as his friends and family leave his apartment for the last time. "This was your first home. And it was a happy place, filled with love and laughter. But more important, because of rent control, it was a friggin' steal!" September 22nd 2019 marked a quarter of a century since the *Friends* gang made their debut on NBC. Their floppy haircuts, enormous phones and quaint dating rituals belong to a distant past, in which coffee was seldom pumpkin-spiced and people jotted down their contact details on napkins. Yet somehow, decades on, the happy place that Chandler describes – and the 236 episodes of love and laughter that occurred there – remains the world's favourite location for an evening's entertainment.

For proof of the enduring charm of *Friends*, consider that in late 2018 Netflix paid the programme's owner, WarnerMedia, about $100m for the right to stream it for the next 12 months. That is not far shy of the $130m that it reportedly spent producing *The Crown*, its most expensive original show. Netflix is secretive with its data, but estimates from Nielsen, a research firm, suggest that *Friends* was the second-most-watched programme among American subscribers in 2018, with an average of more than 20 episodes per account. In Britain figures released by Ofcom, a broadcasting watchdog, disclose that twice as many people watch the comedy on Netflix as stream any other show on any other service. And data from Google reveal that *Friends* is the world's most searched-for sitcom. Other sitcoms released since *Friends* finished have briefly overtaken it, including *The Office*, *How I Met Your Mother* and *The Big Bang Theory*. But eventually viewers break up with them, and return to the gang in Central Perk. What has made the popularity of *Friends* so long-lasting?

The show is funny, but no more so than its rivals. Critics often point out that *Seinfeld* is more sophisticated in the way that it contorts everyday situations into hilarious episodes. The

Not on a break
Google searches for selected American sitcoms, worldwide
100=largest annual search volume

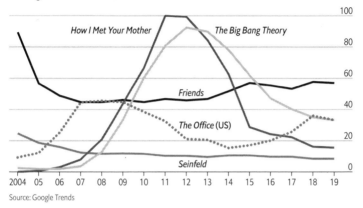

Source: Google Trends

cringe-inducing interactions of a boss and his employees in *The Office* induce more belly laughs. By contrast, *Friends* gets most of its gags from its characters' foibles: a pretentious one (Ross), a vain one (Rachel), an insecure one (Chandler), an uptight one (Monica), a stupid one (Joey) and an eccentric one (Phoebe). Plenty of sitcoms before and since have relied on such a clash of personalities to make the audience chuckle. Where *Friends* stands out is its ability to make viewers care about its characters. It achieved this partly by weaving them together romantically. The decade-long "will-they-won't-they" intrigue between Ross and Rachel at times turned the comedy into a soap opera. Chandler and Monica began the show as acquaintances and ended it as spouses and parents.

But the scriptwriters did not merely develop these relationships over the series' ten years. The best-reviewed episodes on IMDb, a ratings website, tend to be those which delved into the past: either through flashbacks, recovered videotapes (remember those?) or interactions with parents. By the time the last episode aired in 2004, the 50m Americans who tuned in had learned almost everything there was to know about the six characters. (The strength of the series finale, which has the highest rating on IMDb of any episode, has undoubtedly helped its legacy.) The other great appeal of *Friends* is its idealistic portrait of 20-something life. Yet none of the characters spends much time at work, or worries too keenly about their income. The rent control that Chandler describes in the final episode is rarely mentioned, but it means that Monica can pay $200 a month for her flat in the West Village, rather than the estimated $8,000 it would cost today. All the characters have exciting romantic lives – and with much funnier and more attractive partners than the audience could ever hope for.

This is surely why the show continues to find new, young fans. A survey in 2019 of British children aged 9 to 16 found that *Friends* was their favourite series, even though most of them were born after the final episode aired. What could be more captivating than a vision of your future in which you are no longer weighed down by school, but instead spend most of your time larking around with close friends in an enormous apartment, while Brad Pitt, Bruce Willis, Julia Roberts and Reese Witherspoon flit in and out of your lives? That said, some aspects of *Friends* have aged badly. A few jokes about gay characters now seem clumsily homophobic, and Chandler's father, a trans woman, is often used as a punchline. But the warmth that the writing offers viewers in search of light entertainment after an enervating day has endured. They'll be there for you.

Why escape rooms are booming

Most entertainment venues, like cinemas and bowling alleys, go out of their way to identify and illuminate emergency exits. Escape rooms, in which paying participants are locked in a room and must solve puzzles against the clock to secure their release, are explicitly about not having an easy way out. How did escape rooms, a relatively new and niche business, increase in popularity so quickly across the world?

The first escape room is believed to have opened in Japan in 2007. But there were several sources of inspiration behind the idea, says Mink Ette, an escape-room designer based in Britain. The first escape rooms in Japan were inspired by computer games in which participants had to perform a puzzle to escape from an imaginary locked room. In America some of the first escape rooms were based on haunted houses, a popular attraction at funfairs. In eastern Europe the idea first spread as a way of making money out of city-centre basements for which there were few other profitable uses.

Whatever their original inspiration, they have become much more popular in more recent years. In 2014 there were just 22 escape-room venues open in America. Now there are more than 2,300 in that country alone, according to a survey by Room Escape Artist, a website about the industry. In Britain there was just one open at the start of 2013; now there are more than 600. Around the world there are probably over 10,000 escape rooms now in business.

In spite of their rapid increase in numbers, supply has yet to overwhelm the demand. The industry is still very profitable. Some entrepreneurs report that the cost of launching their escape rooms was as little as a few thousand dollars. Would-be escapees often pay premium prices for the experience – around $25–30 for a one-hour game – and with up to 12 participants per hour, the profits add up for a business with low startup and operating costs. David Middleton, co-owner of Bewilder Box, an escape room in Brighton, says that the various groups that visit them – not just gaggles of teenagers but also stag parties, corporate teambuilding events and grandparents taking their families out for the day – keep them filled up all week, ensuring healthy margins. Bigger entertainment companies are also beginning to get in on the game, such as AMC Theatres, a cinema chain that launched escape rooms to promote the release of the latest *Mission: Impossible* film.

Many landlords and local authorities look favourably on the rise of the industry. Landlords can make money from poky offices, shops and basements that are increasingly hard to rent out. Municipalities can help revive fading high streets suffering from the rise of internet shopping, and add things to do for visitors in places not blessed with enough beauty or other attractions to make them hotspots for tourism. But the industry has one big regulatory problem that comes inevitably with locking people in confined spaces: how to comply with fire-safety rules. Many in the industry thought the tragedy in Poland in January 2019, in which five teenage girls died in an escape-room fire in the city of Koszalin, was an accident waiting to happen.

Escape rooms in Britain and America are safer: fire regulations and laws prohibiting kidnap mean that punters cannot be locked in without an alternative means to set themselves free. But that is not true elsewhere in Europe. A survey of escape rooms by Scott Nicholson of the Wilfrid Laurier University in Canada found that 43% of European escape-room players, once locked in, were dependent on staff outside the room. Some venues in eastern Europe even handcuff escapees to the scenery, as part of the challenge. It is no surprise that the Polish government has closed more than a dozen escape rooms for breaches of building regulations since the fire in Koszalin. There are many ways in which escape rooms can be made safer. The installation of panic buttons or magnetic locks that open the door in an emergency is one solution. Making up new games that do not involve locked doors, such as solving a murder, is another. And the use of virtual- and augmented-reality technology, the next frontier in escape-room technology, could make the days of locking players in an actual room a thing of the past.

Is *Die Hard* really a Christmas film?

Die Hard, John McTiernan's skyscraper-set explosion-fest, is lodged firmly in the canon of classic action movies. But should it be included in the canon of Christmas films, too? Some contend that it is in fact the greatest Christmas film of all (take that, *It's a Wonderful Life*). Others object that just because a film is set at Christmas does not make it a Christmas film. The debate has grown so heated that the *Die Hard* Wikipedia page now has a section entitled "Status as a Christmas film". It notes that the 30th-anniversary DVD, released in 2018, included a tongue-in-cheek trailer which sold the film as a heartwarming holiday comedy. But it also notes the lead actor's similarly tongue-in-cheek pronouncement on the matter: "*Die Hard* is not a Christmas movie! It is a goddamn Bruce Willis movie!"

Rewatched in the light of this debate, *Die Hard* does appear to be the cinematic equivalent of a jug of eggnog. It opens with a New York police detective, John McClane (Mr Willis), arriving at Los Angeles International Airport on December 24th. He plans to visit his estranged wife (Bonnie Bedelia) and his young children, and he is carrying a gargantuan teddy bear with a ribbon around its neck. His wife, it should be observed, is named Holly. She is at her office Christmas party on the 30th floor of the Nakatomi Plaza building, where she fends off a colleague's advances by reminding him what day it is: "It's Christmas Eve. Families, stockings, chestnuts? Rudolph and Frosty? Any of these things ring a bell?" Run-DMC's "Christmas In Hollis" blasts on the soundtrack, decorations twinkle in every corner and the plot hinges on whether John and Holly can reconcile in time to open their presents together. What more could you want from a Hollywood Christmas film?

True, the main bearded character is not Santa Claus, but Hans Gruber (Alan Rickman), a suave German criminal mastermind who takes the party-goers hostage while his gang breaks into the company vault. Yet when the first of the bad guys is killed, John plops a Santa hat on the corpse's head, and scrawls a seasonal greeting on its grey sweatshirt: "Now I have a machine-gun. Ho-ho-ho." (You can, of course, now buy sweatshirts printed with that message.) A limousine driver gets to deliver a closing line to rival Tiny Tim's: "If this is their idea of Christmas, I gotta be here for New Year's!" All of this explains the popularity of the internet meme and slogan: "It's not Christmas until Hans Gruber falls from the Nakatomi Tower."

Yet is Christmas really integral to the screenplay, which was adapted by Jeb Stuart and Steven E. de Souza from *Nothing Lasts Forever*, a novel by Roderick Thorp? Wouldn't the siege have been just as exciting if John had visited Holly for Thanksgiving? He doesn't defeat Hans by being generous, or Christian, or family-minded. He does it by being tough, resourceful and capable of swinging through a plate-glass window with a fire-hose knotted around his waist. Judging by its themes and its narrative thrust, declare the naysayers, *Die Hard* is not a Christmas film after all. So who is right?

You can see why critics have found it so difficult to reach a consensus. The anti-Christmas faction points out that the film's original release date was July 1988, and so it is fundamentally a summer blockbuster. The pro-Christmas faction counters that *Miracle on 34th Street* came out in June 1947. The anti-Christmasites protest that no film relating to peace on earth and goodwill to men should depict quite so many people being shot in the chest. The pro-Christmasites' answer: well, there was nothing jolly about the Massacre of the Innocents, either. The ultimate litmus test for a Christmas film, however, is: does it feel strange to watch it at another time of year? For *Die Hard*, the answer is plainly no. It is a good film to watch at any time of year – including at Christmas. But that does not make it a Christmas film.

Contributors

THE EDITOR WISHES to thank the authors and data journalists who created the explainers and accompanying graphics on which this book is based:

Miranda Aldersley, Helen Atkinson, Nicholas Barber, John Bleasdale, Aryn Braun, Will Brown, Joel Budd, Geoff Carr, Slavea Chankova, Farah Cheah, Philip Coggan, Rachel Dobbs, Sarah Donilon, Doug Dowson, Madelaine Drohan, Matthieu Favas, Bo Franklin, James Fransham, Martín González, Lane Greene, Ellen Halliday, Michael Hann, Shakeel Hashim, Evan Hensleigh, John Hooper, Mike Jakeman, Alok Jha, Idrees Kahloon, Abhishek Kumar, Jack Lahart, Ana Lankes, Sarah Leo, Natasha Loder, John McDermott, Matt McLean, Claire McQue, Adam Meara, Leo Mirani, Elliott Morris, Emma O'Kelly, Lloyd Parker, Rosamund Pearce, Sophie Pedder, Lizzy Peet, Nick Pelham, Charles Read, Martin Rivers, Aman Rizvi, Adam Roberts, Dan Rosenheck, Marie Segger, Alex Selby-Boothroyd, Kassia St Clair, Stephanie Studer, James Tozer, Vijay Vaitheeswaran, Andrea Valentino, Charlie Wells, Eleanor Whitehead, Aaron Wiener, Maria Wilczek, Christine Zhang and Wade Zhou.

Index